Is It Love Or Is It Sex?

Why Relationships Don't Work

Carla Wills-Brandon

AN AUTHORS GUILD BACKINPRINT.COM EDITION

Is It Love Or Is It Sex?:
Why Relationships Don't Work
All Rights Reserved © 1989, 2000 by Carla Wills-Brandon

AN AUTHORS GUILD BACKINPRINT.COM EDITION

Published by iUniverse.com, Inc.

For information address:
iUniverse.com, Inc.
620 North 48th Street, Suite 201
Lincoln, NE 68504-3467
www.iuniverse.com

Originally published by Health Communications, Inc

ISBN: 0-595-09350-7

Printed in the United States of America

Dedication

This book is dedicated to my husband Michael, my partner in this life, to my son Aaron, who unknowingly forces me to continue my personal growth process, and to my sister Lila, to whom I can say, "We finally have a healthy relationship."

Acknowledgments

No creation has only one creator. Many people are responsible for making this book possible. Though many have contributed to these pages, I would specifically like to say a special thank you to a few.

I would first of all like to acknowledge and thank Ms. Rita Baker and all of her fingers for typing the original manuscript. I would like to express my gratitude to Marie Stilkind for going to bat with Health Communications for this manuscript.

I would also like to commend my family for putting up with me while I was working on this book. I would like to thank my husband Michael and my son Aaron for their support and patience. I tend to become "that grouchy person" (as I refer to myself) at times, while writing.

Last but not least, I would like to express my deepest gratitude to all of the men and women who have had the courage to break the No Talk Rule about their own dysfunctional sexual history, sexuality and painful experience with relationships. Without their courage, this book would never have become a reality.

Contents

Preface

There are numerous books on shelves all over the world which discuss in depth such topics as what makes a relationship work, why relationships don't succeed, sex in the marital relationship, sex and the single person and so on. I believe there are more definitions and solutions provided by authors, helping professionals, institutions and schools of thought to the question, "What makes a healthy relationship?" than for any other major issue facing us today. But even with all of these resources and opinions, the divorce rate in the United States and in Europe continues to be overwhelming. Most of us are still asking ourselves, "What does it take to have a healthy, successful, loving relationship with another human being?"

Humankind has been pondering the topics of love, sex and marriage (or relationships) for centuries. Throughout history, in poetry, fiction and nonfiction, the quest for relief from the frustration and confusion these topics produce is evident. Recently I was with a group of men and women, young and old, married and single, with various backgrounds, who were all in recovery from addictions — to alcohol, drugs, food, sex, workaholism, co-dependency and the like. The topic of discussion in the group was, "What is love?"

Well, of course, with such a diverse group there were many, many definitions of love. As a matter of fact, there were as many definitions as there were people. No two were the same. Some of these definitions were:

Love is a feeling of connection with the whole universe.

Love is giving permission to those around us to be who they are.

Love is respecting someone we want in our lives enough to let them go.

Love is allowing our mates and friends to grow at their own pace, in their own way.

Love is being available to others in time of need with support and concern.

Love is a feeling of warmth inside.

Love is being at peace with everything and everyone around us.

Love is sharing feelings with one another, even when it hurts.

Even though there were many definitions, the final consensus of the group was that there isn't a single description of love, that the feeling of love is a *personal* experience. The group also agreed that the first concept of love comes from one's initial experience within the family of origin.

The group believed that if the family of origin was dysfunctional as a consequence of addiction of any sort or as a result of emotional, physical, sexual or spiritual abuse, then the members of such a family would most likely have a dysfunctional concept of love and not know what a healthy relationship is. Everyone agreed that to experience healthy love and healthy relationships, they had to weed out some, if not all, of the traditions and values they had learned in their original families about love and relationships. Only by doing that could they blossom into individuals who feel connected in a healthy way to self, to others and even to a Higher Power or spiritual concept.

At some point in our lives most of us want to reach out for and have a wholesome relationship with another person. Many of us have, at one time or another, had unhealthy and painful courtships, friendships, love affairs, engagements or marriages. Some of us still feel at a loss in our present associations and move from one to the next, disappointed again and again. We may be connected with someone in a way that feels empty and lonely but we dread abandonment so we stay, hoping for some miracle to improve things but unable to say what kind of miracle is needed.

This book does not tell why we have sick relationships; that answer can only come from within. What this book does is to provide direction and suggestions, ideas the reader may want to consider while seeking his or her own solutions. The second half of the book includes a workbook and some key questions. Your answers to those questions may unlock the doors you need to walk through to attain your personal recovery from dysfunctional relationships. This book is for those of you who are single and ready for a successful intimacy as well as for those of you who are already in a committed relationship but still feel that something is missing.

In 12-Step support groups such as Alcoholics Anonymous, Sex Addicts Anonymous, Co-dependents Anonymous, Adult Children of Alcoholics and others, there is a saying, *Take what you like and leave the rest.* It is my hope that you, the reader, will be able to take from these pages what you feel applies to your life and find your own definition of healthy love. Good luck to you on your path toward healing. Know that success is already with you.

Carla Wills-Brandon

Introduction

Hello! My name is Carla and I am recovering from just about every addiction known to humanity. I have a friend who refers to himself as a dabbler in the world of addictions because he jumped from one addiction to another when confronted with pain, shame and fear. So I guess one might say I'm a recovering dabbler! And yes, this is another one of those books about addictive relationships. But it has a different twist to it.

Michael, my spouse and partner along the path of recovery, and I had been experiencing difficulties in our relationship for years. We are both professional therapists and, way back when, we thought we could solve our problems ourselves. I still tease Michael, saying that I was his dissertation project, in that he married me for the challenge of fixing me. Our relationship didn't improve over time but slowly disintegrated because we were both involved in a number of addictions. These addictions were much more powerful than all of our education, degrees and certifications put together. Eventually we both realized that the disease of chemical dependency had worn us down and that all of the brainpower in the world was no match for what we had been fighting. We admitted defeat and sought help.

Michael and I thought that with treatment for my chemical dependency, our relationship would suddenly snap right into place and, of course, be perfect. Little did we know we were living with denial and deluded thinking. As the identified chemically dependent patient in the family, I felt that I had forced Michael into a caretaker role and I took on total responsibility for the relationship. Neither of us realized that our relationship was a 50-50 deal and that we were equally dysfunctional long before the disease of chemical dependency became an issue for us. Eventually, after each of us had done a great deal of individual family of origin work, we discovered that we had an investment in our respective roles within the relationship. Michael and I realized that it was not by chance that we had married one another. We fit together like a couple of puzzle pieces.

I was invested in my role as the identified patient and Michael was very comfortable with his role as major caretaker. Neither of us knew how to operate outside of those roles. With recovery from chemical dependency, a number of other addictions replaced the dysfunction that drugs and alcohol had brought into the relationship.

These other addictions now had room to breathe and they began to magnify. We went to several therapists for help in our relationship. My role as the identified patient was reinforced. I became the problem that needed fixing during these marriage-counseling sessions and, of course, the center of attention. We would leave the sessions feeling unresolved. During these times Michael seemed to get lost in the shuffle and was viewed as the poor bewildered husband. He would be stroked for "putting up with it all" while we were in the disease of chemical dependency. Then after our therapy sessions, we would argue in the car going down the freeway, all the way home. It was as if therapy created more problems for both of us.

This cycle continued for several years with several therapists. I felt confused and frustrated and Michael was ready to give up on any further therapy. We were both very disillusioned and wondered if we would ever get this relationship straight. I knew that I was getting a payoff for staying in my role as the scapegoat and Michael knew he received strokes for his role as the saintly husband but we also knew that these roles were sabotaging any chance we had for true intimacy. As a recovering couple, Michael and I felt very *stuck*.

Eventually we went our separate ways into family of origin work and began to learn some things that really made a lot of sense. I discovered that I had much unfinished business to attend to and that I needed to learn how to fill myself up from within with healthy, rather than unhealthy, behavior. Being the scapegoat in the relationship was my unhealthy way of getting my need for attention taken care of, even if that attention was negative. Michael discovered that he needed just as much help as I did. He realized that by focusing on my dysfunction, he did not have the time to look too closely at his own unfinished business. He also found out that his role as the saintly husband kept him from discovering the pleasures of being an imperfect human being. Michael jokingly says today that when he appeared very much in control on the outside, he was usually a screaming chaotic mess on the inside.

When we began our recovery as a couple, I realized that the more perfect he seemed on the outside, the more pain he was experiencing on the inside. When I would come home and see that the house, the yard and the cars were all picture-perfect, I knew something was going on in Michael's recovery. As he has continued his recovery process, he has become more relaxed around the house, in the yard and he even allows the cars to become messy. I finally had to hire a housekeeper and a gardener because in recovery, the house and the yard were falling apart.

Since neither of us knew how to communicate in a healthy manner, we each had to become responsible in finding out how to do that. This included learning how to disagree and confront one another fairly. We did not know that disagreement and confrontation were normal in a relationship. Neither of us knew the first thing about fair fighting. Our disagreements were rarely resolved because we didn't know how to work them through and we thought that resolution was about someone winning. Wrong! We had to learn that it was all right for us to have different beliefs and ideas and that we were not always going to agree. I had to learn how to respect Michael enough to allow him to have a different opinion and he had to learn how to do the same.

Today Michael and I are in recovery for our addictions and believe we are equally responsible for the relationship. We have some tools that allow us to have the honest intimacy we both longed for and we have developed some skills that allow for disagreement. I am totally responsible for myself within the relationship, as he is for himself. He is not responsible for making me a complete and whole person, nor can he focus on me as a way of distracting from his own recovery work. We are continuing to learn how to respect one another's need for boundaries and personal space, both physically and emotionally. It has taken us 12 years to get to where we are and we continue to work on the relationship one day at a time.

Several years back, Michael and I decided to see just how healthy our relationship was by going into private practice together. During the first year, the survival of our marriage was at times questionable and today it is obvious that without recovery, the practice would have gone quickly downhill. To say it has been hard would be minimizing the amount of personal growth we were both forced into during that first year of being in practice together. We had to work harder on our relationship as a recovering couple and we had to develop our own separate selves, apart from the office. The experience encouraged us to continue the process of self-discovery.

In our practice I work mainly with women and Michael works with men and children. I believe, as a professional, that for me to work with men would be a disservice to them. I am not always able to see clearly what is going on with a male client because I have not had the experience of being male. Michael holds the same view with regard to himself in working with females. Some professionals disagree with this philosophy but for us, it seems to work.

When a couple comes to our office for marital counseling, Michael and I see them together. We discovered some time back that a couple with one therapist was in an awkward situation because one member of the relationship usually felt like the odd person out. Counseling couples as a couple has been very therapeutic. Besides, it seems to make more sense.

Over the years we have counseled together with many couples in dysfunctional relationships. During this time we have seen that there really aren't any quick fixes or answers etched in stone. The dysfunction within the relationship is always specific to the couple's family of origin issues. It has been interesting to see how the men in the relationships we work with communicate the way their fathers did with their mothers, while the women communicate the way their mothers did with their fathers.

Since we work with many individuals in recovery from chemical dependency, co-dependency, eating disorders, sexual addiction and other problems, we have noticed that as one addiction is dealt with, another arises. Couples working hard on their personal recovery process would be frustrated at the lack of resolution of the dysfunction in the relationship. It was as if recovery created more problems for these recovering couples. Intimacy did not improve and communication became more of a problem. Sexual problems emerged and the shame associated with the issue of sexuality would force the relationship into even more dysfunctional co-dependency. Co-dependency is the result of growing up in dysfunctional families where it isn't safe to talk about what is going on, to feel certain feelings or to trust the perceptions from the environment. Below are some behaviors that couples get into as a result of their individual family of origin issues.

Earmarks Of A Co-dependent Relationship

- Feeling that your partner owes you something. *I'm going to stay here and get mine because he (or she) owes me, after all I've done.*
- Selection of improbable partners.
- Arrogance about the relationship.

- Intense exaggeration in the relationship. Obsession with the other person and expectation of the same level of feeling in return. *Do you think about me as much as I think about you?*
- Little spontaneous playfulness.
- Too many fixed requirements and objectives.
- Loss or devaluation of individual differences.
- Too little or too much time devoted to the relationship.
- Lack of conflict resolution.
- Too much self-control and too many censored feelings. Wariness about what is expressed. No sharing of feelings or vulnerability.
- Fear of exploring things together. Lack of experimentation.
- One or both partners have a myth of their own perfection or the other's.
- Sense of being one-down or one-up in the relationship.
- No Talk Rules. Less and less talk about what is going on.
- Belief that the other person defines who you are.
- Caution about making a commitment in the relationship or regret about having made one.
- Preoccupation with the partner.
- Energy swings — cycles of fitness and energy followed by periods of exhaustion, even to the point of illness or depression.
- Upheaval and chaos in the relationship.
- Sacrificing outside things for the sake of the relationship.
- Use of substitutes (drugs, sex, food, etc.) to avoid intimacy.
- Nurturing and caretaking take the place of shared intimacy.

CoSA Newcomer Packet

Since one of my main interests in the field of addictions is eating disorders, I have worked with many women who suffer from forms of bulimia, obsessive-compulsive eating and anorexia. Many of them are recovering from other addictions and have suffered some type of trauma as a member of a dysfunctional family. One of Michael's interests in the field of recovery is sexual addiction. Because of this, he works with a large number of male sexual addicts. Most are recovering from other addictions and find they have difficulty with issues of sexuality. While working with our individual caseloads and doing couples work together, we both began seeing behavior patterns which are common among couples in recovery. The co-dependent behaviors were there and very obvious but the dysfunction, for many couples, went much deeper. For some couples, the dysfunction seemed to involve a relationship between eating disorders and sexual addiction.

1

Sex And Food: How They Work Together

Sex and food. Both are necessary for the continuation of our species. Both are very powerful and have the capacity to change the way we feel about our lives and the world around us. If used in an addictive manner, food and sex can distort our reality just as effectively as alcohol and other drugs, and the consequences of addiction to food and sex can be just as devastating as alcoholism or drug dependency.

Many people in our society escape the realities of life by hanging out in front of the refrigerator when facing the problems of being an adult in our world. As I described in my earlier book, *Eat Like A Lady: Guide For Overcoming Bulimia* (Health Communications, 1989), eating disorders are survival skills that have enabled many of us to function and they come from our dysfunctional families. As a bulimic I could insulate myself from pain, shame and other feelings with food. Food allowed me to escape the feelings I had as a child and as an adult, it provided me with a false sense of security. But as

1

with all addictions, my eating disorder backfired by protecting me from reality. While in addiction, I never learned how to live life in the real world. I never really grew up.

Many individuals escape the world of reality through fantasy relationships. The fantasy of what a relationship should be is an illusion based on sexual acting out. Sex replaces intimacy, giving the relationship a false sense of well-being. When sex diminishes or is not an intense part of a relationship, the perception is that the relationship is bad. *If we have good sex, we have a good relationship. Sex will make it better.* These ideas belong to the cycle of sexual addiction. The sexual acting out becomes the fix, just as alcohol is the illusionary fix for the alcoholic.

More and more information has begun to surface on sexual addiction, starting with Patrick Carnes' book, *Out of the Shadows.* He describes three levels of sexual addiction and discusses how each affects the addict's ability to perceive the world as it really is. Each level has a set of specific characteristics and behaviors which interfere with the ability to establish healthy, intimate relationships with the self or others.

Our Shaming Myths

As a society, we have a lot of shame around issues of sexuality and we believe a number of myths associated with appropriate versus inappropriate sexual behavior.

I was watching a talk show on television recently when the discussion was about what the legal consequences should be for an adult woman who had sex with a teenaged boy. Half of the participating television audience thought the sex act between the adult woman and minor boy was all right. They stated further that the boy had consented to the sexual act by not saying no to the adult woman. They argued that he must have wanted to have sex with the woman because he didn't say no and that he probably learned a lot about sex. The other half of the audience (the side I applauded) stated that this was a form of sexual abuse, that the teenager did not have the maturity to stand up to the adult and say no. They further argued that as an authority figure (as an adult), the woman was in a position of power over the young boy, making it impossible for him to say no.

I cheered those who saw this incident as one of sexual abuse but was saddened at the same time. I was amazed at the amount of conflict in the audience over this issue. I was also surprised at the lack of information among the majority of these people regarding basic child development and sexuality. It impressed upon me the extent of sexual abuse in our society that is based on ignorance. At the core of sexual addiction, as with all other addictions, is the dysfunctional family system.

I believe that society as a whole plays a large part in perpetuating family system dysfunction and many of the ad-dictions we see today. It is still important to look good, be positive and not talk about unpleasant things, even at the expense of our emotional well-being. For many who have eating disorders, losing weight at any cost to fit society's dictum that thin is beautiful or thin is sexy can be life-threatening. Anorexics will starve themselves to dangerously low body weights to be perfect. Exercise bulimics will jog, pump iron and exercise past their bodies' endurance, injuring joints and bones, to fit in and be beautiful. Our society reflects this point of view in newspaper ads, magazines and television. As a result, children as young as nine and ten are obsessed with their bodies and with fear of being fat.

I know of a nine-year-old whose mother told her she was too fat and put her on a diet. This child, in my opinion, was weight appropriate. Her mother had her counting calories and keeping a list of what she ate. This weight appropriate child believed she was fat.

In our society, we also expect our children to grow up too quickly. This too is reflected in the media, where sex is the name of the game in rock music videos and in advertisements where having a pimple is a sin. Young people are experiment-ing with sex at earlier ages, but contraception and sex educa-tion are still in the closet in many parts of the country. As a result, pregnancies are common among all races, religions and social positions. With AIDS on the rise, we are finally being forced to make some decisions about confronting sexuality among our youth. We are finally doing this from an educational standpoint rather than the way we did in the past when sexual messages were based in shame.

We, as a society, spend many dollars on products to make us smell sexy, taste sexy, look sexy, feel sexy and act sexy. We have grapefruit diets, liquid diets, pills, shots, wired jaw and surgical procedures for weight reduction to guarantee a beautiful, sexy body. As a culture, we are beginning to develop an obsession for exercise. Exercise gyms are filling up as they never have before. Even gyms use sex as a way of selling memberships. *Before you primp, you've got to pump some iron*. Beautiful, well-proportioned, scantily dressed women make such comments while lifting weights, reinforcing that in order to be acceptable, one has to buy the fantasy.

The Illusion

How does all this affect our concept of what a relationship should be? Do we really know what intimacy is or are we looking for the perfect illusion? How many of us open our monthly department store bills to find advertisements for women's nightgowns and undergarments? Who are these ads directed at, or should I say, who in the average American family usually opens these bills? In newspaper and magazine advertisements, we find that sex sells everything from chewing gum for "that sexy smile," to cars for those looking for "a sleek, sexy look." Not only are females used as sex objects to entice the male buyer but since the women's liberation movement, well-built, perfectly proportioned, sexy males sell perfume "to drive him mad" and blue jeans "that will drive her mad" to our female population.

The truth about all the advertising that uses sex as a hook into the buyer is that it is not the gum, perfume, blue jeans or car that is being sold. What is being sold is a fantasy — the products just happen to be part of the fantasy, the illusion of perfection, and we, as a society, have bought it.

Men learn to look for that perfect woman and women learn to look for that perfect man. So, many of us look for the fantasy relationship because we believe that is the way things are supposed to be. How many of us are really content with our bodies, our mates, our lives? How many of us strive for the fantasy of perfection in hopes that we will some day be happy with who we are? How many of us, as one perfume advertisement put it, really do want to "share the fantasy" with someone we think will make us feel complete?

Many of us walk around feeling inadequate, lonely and empty. We use food, sex, drugs, alcohol, work, religion, relationships and more to cover up our feelings of insecurity and inner shame. We have a horrible fear of people finding out just how imperfect we are so we are constantly looking for that one drink, drug or relationship that will fill us up and make us feel whole. We know almost nothing about what true, honest, intimate communication with others or even self is all about because nobody ever taught us that it was okay to talk about our hurt, shame and anger. Most of us are totally unaware that we need to learn how to fill ourselves up from within before we can experience a healthy relationship with another human being.

As a society we are obsessed with looking good on the outside, moving forward financially and keeping up with the neighbors. It is as if we believe that when we accomplish these goals, somehow our feelings about who we are will get fixed. But I believe many of us are suffering on the inside and feeling very inadequate and wondering why. Many of us are divorcing, having life crises, living in loveless relationships and feeling unsatisfied. Or we are settling for second best by not doing what we really want to do because of fear and lack of confidence in who we are. Maybe we are in a relationship that just isn't working and we feel as though we are missing some great secret about life and love. And on top of it all, we cannot get this thing called *life* right.

2

A Couple In Trouble

The following describes a relationship some of us may relate to.

Joyce's Story

Joyce grew up with an alcoholic father and a mother who worked at always trying to keep the family together and running smoothly. Her father would come home from work, eat dinner and retire to the living room to drink a couple of beers and watch television. He did this five nights a week and on weekends he would spend his time out in the garage, working on various projects. Joyce tried as a child to win some attention from her father by making straight A's in school but could never seem to please him. At times she thought he just didn't like her.

Her mother would try to make it up to Joyce and her brother by taking them shopping or baking treats. Joyce couldn't understand why her mother wouldn't do something to *fix* her father. She rarely saw them hug one another or display any intimacy. She knew they slept in separate beds and could never imagine them having a sexual relationship. She often wondered how they ever conceived her. Joyce also noticed that when her mother seemed angry or hurt, she would sit alone and eat. She remembers one late night when her mother ate half of a chocolate cake. The confusing thing about the family was that, although Joyce rarely saw her parents fight, she still felt there was something wrong.

Joyce promised herself she would find someone who loved and cared for her. She also promised herself she would find someone to fill those needs that had never been fulfilled by her father. Joyce's father wasn't a sloppy drunk, he just seemed emotionally numb and unavailable when he drank. Joyce decided she would find someone who would be there when she needed to talk and she fantasized about how there would never be silence in her relationship with her dream man.

After several dysfunctional relationships with men who not only acted like her father but also looked like him, she met John. John didn't have any of the characteristics her father had as far as she could tell and this pleased her no end. He was attentive, charming and said just the right thing at the right time. She believed she was in love and felt she had found the answer for the emptiness she felt.

John bought her pretty things and didn't seem to have a problem with spending money on her the way her father did. They eventually began a sexual relationship and Joyce noted that John liked sex a lot and was glad for this since she believed her parents had problems with sex. She didn't want her relationship with John to be like theirs! She also noticed that John did like to drink a bit but his behavior didn't seem to be affected by it the way her father's was. They decided to get married and Joyce believed that now, well taken care of and secure, she would live happily ever after. Little did she know her happiness would fade quickly.

Several years into the marriage, John was drinking more and more. Joyce noticed that they did not talk with one another the way they used to. They still had sex quite often and Joyce was grateful for that because lately having sex was the only time she felt connected with him. Once in a while

John would buy her something nice when she complained about feeling all alone.

Over the years, Joyce began to feel incomplete in her relationship with John and would nibble on sweets when she felt lonely. Her favorite food to treat herself with was chocolate. When she ate chocolate, she felt as though she had just received a hug. Several years down the line, Joyce knew she had put on quite a bit of weight, just like her mother. Out of fear of becoming like mother, she decided to go to therapy and work on herself.

She wanted to find out what she needed to do to make John happy again. She felt she had tried everything and nothing worked. Even their sex life had gone downhill. They seemed to have sex only about once a month and even then there wasn't any love. She felt he didn't love her anymore, though she tried to keep the relationship going. He said he wanted her to have a child and she did. He said he wanted her to go to work and she did. He said he wanted her to grow her hair longer and she did. He asked her to do certain things for him sexually and, even though she felt uncomfortable about it, she did them, hoping that would make him happy.

Her therapist asked about her childhood, seemed acutely interested in her father's alcoholism, talked about how living with an alcoholic parent can sear one for life, said this experience was still affecting her and referred her to a Family Awareness Program on the Disease of Alcoholism. Not only did Joyce receive information about her father's disease but she also began to see that her husband had the same disease. She joined a support group for family members of alcoholics called Al-Anon and learned that she was not responsible for her husband's behavior. Joyce learned how to change her behavior to make John more responsible for his. After a year or so, John's drinking began to cause problems in all areas of his life, including his job. His supervisor at work asked him to submit to a chemical dependency evaluation. John scored high on the evaluation for possible alcoholism and was asked to participate in an outpatient alcohol recovery program. John had known for some time that alcohol was becoming a problem and agreed to what his supervisor suggested. Joyce was ecstatic. She believed this treatment process would return John to being the man she had married and that all her problems would be solved. She really believed that when he got *fixed,* he would be there for her once again. Little did she know that this was the beginning of a long, hard road to self-discovery for both of them.

Recovery was hard for John because alcohol had become his best friend and helped him solve a lot of problems. It allowed him to relax after a hard day's work and helped him to suppress his feelings of sadness and anger. Now that he was sober, he felt he didn't know how to function in life comfortably because the alcohol, which had cushioned him from reality, was gone. He became very involved in his support groups at the outpatient treatment program and active in Alcoholics Anonymous. He attended support meetings every night and was quickly making many new friends.

Joyce, watching all this, began to feel left out of his life even more than before his recovery. She thought this might be temporary and that John would soon return to her. They were having sex more often but Joyce felt unsatisfied and, at times, angry because their sex life was so mechanical. But she feared driving him back to drinking so she didn't say anything to upset him.

During the first year of recovery John stayed sober but Joyce continued to have a weight problem. The emptiness she carried inside, which she had thought marriage to John would fix, was growing larger. She found herself standing in front of the pantry more often, looking for something to eat. She was always so hungry. Her hunger was not for food but for the love and attention she never received from her father. Now she couldn't seem to get it from her husband either.

As time went by, John continued to stay sober but was always either working or at meetings. Sex had become minimal. Joyce began to wonder if John was having an affair with someone at one of his meetings. She had a lot of anger toward John but didn't express it for fear he would leave her. So she stuffed her feelings with food and also began to go on shopping sprees, hoping that would fill up her emptiness.

John was confused. He was grateful for his sobriety and loved his support groups. He felt the people there accepted him for who he was and he didn't have to prove his worth. He wished Joyce could do the same and stop being so demanding. He was angry with her because she was so needy, just like his mother. He realized that when he was around Joyce, he felt suffocated. John had discovered that he could share anything in his support groups and be supported, while with Joyce he felt he always had to be strong and together for her. When he did try to share his feelings, she shamed him by saying he shouldn't feel that way. He had trouble showing his anger around her because when he did, she cried. His mother was emotional and John always felt it was his fault. He felt the same way with Joyce. Even if he was angry about something that had nothing to do with Joyce, she still cried. John saw Joyce as very self-centered, like a big, needy sponge. He felt that no matter what he did, it was never enough.

John's Story

John had grown up with a workaholic father who was rarely home. John was the oldest of three sons and became surrogate parent to his younger brothers in the father's absence. He knew that his father had an affair with someone at the workplace for many years. What had always confused him was that his mother never figured it out. He had a lot of sadness about his relationship with his father.

He felt he was cheated out of a father-son relationship because of his father's affair. Also, in the father's absence, his mother would complain to him about her life. She shared with him things he would just as soon not hear about. It was as if it was not all right for John to just be a kid. His mother and father fought a lot behind closed doors but John and his brothers could always hear them.

John would feel scared during these times because there was always a lot of yelling when his parents fought. Sometimes his father just left, slamming the door on his way out. John always feared his father would leave for good. His mother would cry all night. Sometimes John would get out of bed to make sure she was all right and then she would hug him and cry. John felt it was his job to make her happy and he really worked hard at it.

He noticed that his mother sometimes took some little yellow pills. When she took these, she seemed to be in a better mood but would forget things. John felt as though he was his mother's parent instead of her being his parent. To this day, John's mother called him when she was in pain or when she wanted to discuss his father.

John also had anger toward his father for leaving him and his mother and going off for long periods of time. He felt that his father left him the job of taking care of his mother. John knew that this was not supposed to be his responsibility. He knew his father did this because he couldn't deal with her himself and he felt angry that his father wasn't more responsible.

When John was first introduced to Joyce by a college friend, he was amazed at how independent she seemed. He was impressed with her positive attitude toward life and in her company, he felt appreciated for himself. He didn't feel he had to take care of her because she seemed so capable of caring for herself. She was really interested in him as a person and didn't seem to want anything from him except to enjoy his company.

John thought at the time that this was his perfect fantasy woman come to life. He noticed that she had a tendency to put on a few pounds now and then, but in general she seemed very much in control of her life. The last thing he wanted for a mate was a needy, out-of-control woman like his mother. When they started having a sexual relationship, John noticed that Joyce was pretty inexperienced but decided that was all right. And in some ways he really liked that quality about her. They married and John felt he was finally on the road to a life of his own, completely different and separate from that of his parents.

Over the years, John saw that Joyce put on more weight and was not taking care of herself the way she used to. She was becoming more needy and John was feeling engulfed by her. She seemed so unhappy and she expected him to make her feel better. Joyce's need for attention was so overwhelming that it seemed to suck the life force out of him. Her crying made him feel angry and out of control. At times John would leave the house and go to the convenience store to get a couple of beers. He also noticed that his drinking had increased over the years but didn't think much about it. He decided that if anyone had a wife like Joyce, they would drink, too.

For him, sex with Joyce was a nightmare. She was very critical and his anger toward her would emerge during their lovemaking. Afterward he would be ashamed for being so mechanical and cold during their sexual encounters. More and more he would have sex with himself by masturbating. Sex with self became emotionally safer than sex with Joyce.

He had a great deal of support from the Alcoholics Anonymous groups. Here, people accepted him for himself and he felt supported. The people in these groups talked about things he wouldn't share with Joyce. Every night he went either to outpatient treatment or to support groups. John really believed he had found the answer. He wondered why Joyce had dropped out of her support groups. He tried to talk to her about it a couple of times but she didn't seem interested. He brought it up with his treatment group and the feedback he received from them was that he was not responsible for her. Also, John had thought that as a result of his treatment, Joyce would begin to lose weight but she was eating more than ever. Sex with Joyce was almost nonexistent now and John was having sex with himself more often. He also discovered that masturbation could relieve him of a lot of stressful feelings.

At his meetings there were a couple of women who were very nice to him and, though his sponsor in AA told him to stay away from the women, he fantasized about them a lot. A couple of times he thought of having an affair, but he did not want to be like his father so he decided against that. But he did enjoy talking with women and sharing his problems with them. He felt safer with the women than the men. John wished Joyce were this easy to talk to. With these women, John felt he was getting some needs taken care of that were not met by Joyce. He shared things with them that he would never share with his wife. When they phoned him at home, he felt uncomfortable because Joyce seemed angry and jealous.

John couldn't understand why Joyce was so upset about his relationships with other women and he told her so. She accused him of having an affair and he said he was not sleeping with them. Joyce's response was, "Well, you might as well be." John went to the bathroom to masturbate his feelings away while Joyce grabbed a couple of bags of potato chips and locked herself away in the bedroom to eat and watch television.

John thought that their problems were the result of Joyce's self-centered behavior and Joyce felt they were the result of John's uncaring attitude. Who was right? Who was responsible for the problems in this relationship? More important, what issues did they need to address individually? How were their family of origin issues keeping them from intimacy with one another? And, last but not least, what addictions were active in this relationship? How did sex help John avoid his feelings? What did food do for Joyce's painful feelings? How did John's sexual addiction affect Joyce? How did Joyce's addiction to food affect John? What exactly is sexual addiction and how is it related to eating disorders?

3

Fear Of Growing Up:
The Family Of Origin Impact

As I've said, my addictions or "dabbling" kept me from growing up and facing reality. I had a fear of growing up because I did not have the tools for living in the adult world. I believe any addiction is really about fear of growing up. To remain childlike is to avoid pain, sadness and responsibility for self. Also to remain in childhood is to avoid confronting unfinished business with our family of origin. If we remain childlike as a result of addiction, we will also be stunted developmentally in our own emotional growth process. To be stunted in our emotional growth keeps us from continuing the developmental process toward self-discovery. The life process is about self-discovery. We learn who we are by resolving those issues that cause difficulty, both past and present. As we continue to work through these learning situations that life presents, we also learn how to conquer our fears and develop a greater understanding of self, of others and of our purpose in life. Addiction keeps us from moving through our fears and becomes a temporary bandage for the difficulties we experience in daily life. As a result of addiction, many of us are losing out on opportunities for growth and self-discovery.

The Veil Of Addiction

Addiction also keeps us from healing within because we cannot thoroughly experience our grief, rage, pain or even joy. The veil of addiction blunts our feelings so that we do not experience reality as it is. All our feelings are necessary for our growth and to avoid some, if not all of them, is to avoid life. Our feelings motivate us to grow and change. They also give us the courage to risk and explore. If a family system is safe and secure, children become adults who feel safe and secure enough to risk, grow, explore and change. They have healthy skills which enable them to protect and care for themselves in the adult world.

If a family system is dysfunctional in any way, the children within the system do not feel safe nor supported enough to risk, grow, explore and change. They grow into fearful adults with inadequate coping skills. Our first concept of what the world is like comes from growing up in our families. If our families are safe and secure, we learn that the world outside is exciting. If we grow up in families that are unsafe because of emotional, physical or sexual abuse, we learn that the world is scary. Many of us, because of our family of origin experiences in childhood, fear our feelings, fear change, fear ourselves, fear others, fear our world and continue to hide in illusion with addiction.

From now on, we will be discussing sexual addiction in terms of its effect on the developmental process toward self-discovery. Discussion of its specific characteristics will be limited because that would take up an entire book and one has already been written on this. For more in-depth information about sexual addiction, one may refer to Patrick Carnes' work titled, *Out Of The Shadows*. Carnes discusses the specifics of the disease of sexual addiction and provides research information which substantiates his findings. The information on sexual addiction in the following pages will be directed to its effects in relation to self, to others and to spiritual development. We will also take a closer look at the origins of sexual addiction, along with its connection to eating disorders.

Earlier we discussed how our society is obsessed with living the perfect fantasy in order to escape the realities of life. Some have even referred to this as the American dream. Sexual addiction is one way to enter the world of fantasy, apparently a way that is often used. One has only to go as far as the corner convenience store and see the number of pornographic magazines on the racks to be aware of the level of sexual addiction in our society. A trip to the local video store reveals a booming backroom business in triple X-rated pornographic movies. The video recorder has reduced the shame associated with watching X-rated movies. The dread of being caught going into an X-rated movie theater is less because now these films can be viewed in the privacy of one's home. Our media reflects those trends that have taken hold in our society and what the media is telling us is that sexual addiction is alive and well.

Sex Addiction: Often Hidden, Seldom Harmless

Is sexual addiction about being an immoral, weak-willed person? For years society at large saw all alcoholics as bad, weak-willed and immoral. Some still hold this point of view even though more than 30 years ago the American Medical Association determined that alcoholism is a disease. Many alcoholics while in their disease do behave badly and act out in immoral ways but with the help of Alcoholics Anonymous and alcohol treatment centers, millions have reached recovery from their addictions and have become responsible for their behavior. Many individuals are sexually addicted and have committed extremely offensive crimes against others. Their behavior is unacceptable and they need to be held accountable for it. But there are also many whose sexual acting out has not caused any legal consequences. Many sexual addicts never have to leave their homes or their significant relationships to act out their addiction. All they have to do is enter the

fantasy that lives within and temporarily escape. Their consequences are stunted emotional growth, a lack of intimacy
with others, sexual dysfunction, dysfunction within their current family and a lot of self-hate. Just as all alcoholics are not
skid row bums, not all sex addicts are abusive offenders.

As I've noted, many condone some forms of child abuse
and many have little awareness of what is sexually abusive.
Abused children may develop one of two attitudes toward the
world. They can see themselves as victims who cannot protect
themselves and continue to be abused by others or they may
see themselves as offenders who will hurt others before they
can get hurt themselves. Abusive behavior produces individuals who do not know how to protect themselves and it
produces individuals who continue the cycle of pain by
abusing others. I believe sexual addiction is a result of sexually abusive behavior. The acorn does not fall far from the
tree. Sexual addiction appears to be intergenerational in that
the behaviors are passed on from one generation to the next.

A Broad Definition

*For our purposes we will use a very basic definition of
what sexually addictive behavior is. For us, sexually addictive
behavior is defined as any continuously repeated sexual
behavior, expressed emotionally or physically, with fantasy or
sexual acting out, which keeps a person from feeling feelings
and dealing with reality. If the sexual fantasy or acting out
provides a method of escape regularly, it is sexually addictive.
If the sexual acting out or fantasizing interferes with or
replaces intimacy in a significant sexual relationship, sexual
addiction is evident.*

A healthy adult sexual relationship requires intimacy and
connectedness during sexual encounters. An unhealthy sexual
relationship feels disconnected and sex involves only the
physical act and/or fantasy. The physical act itself or the
fantasy become more important than the intimate union of
two people. Where do our concepts of a relationship come
from? Our family of origin, of course.

We know that our first concept of what makes a relationship comes from watching our parents interact with one another. If our fathers or mothers are addicted to food, work, rage, sex, religion, drugs, alcohol, shopping, worry, relationships or anything else, they have trouble experiencing true intimacy and honest communication. Addictions are the walls that not only separate us from our own self-discovery but also distance us from those around us. If our parents were addicted, that addiction limited their emotional growth and affected their capacity for intimate relationships.

This is not to say that our parents were bad or didn't love us. In some cases they may not have loved us but for the majority, our parents did care. As a result of *their* dysfunctional family of origin upbringing, they did not receive all the tools necessary for a productive emotional life. To blame our parents for our dysfunction is to focus away from ourselves. For our healing, we can hold them accountable for their inappropriate behavior and *have* all our feelings about the way they impacted our lives, but to *blame* them is to stay stuck in the problem. To hold accountable is to move into the solution. If our parents are dysfunctional in any way, they were themselves raised in dysfunctional family systems.

Dysfunction attracts dysfunction or — put another way — birds of a feather flock together. If one parent is dysfunctional, the other is also, no matter how much in control they appear to be. I am always intrigued with the denial that surrounds parental dysfunction. I have heard people say, "Well, my father was awful. He was a drunk, a womanizer and a rager but Mother held it together. She was a saint." In reality, mother *appeared* to be the safer of the two and children need safety to survive, even if only the illusion of safety. So my question is, "If Mother was in control and emotionally together, why did she continue to live in this abusive situation?" Both parents are equally accountable for their behavior while we were growing up. By investigating our family of origin history we can come to a better understanding of ourselves.

4

The Dysfunctional Family's Effect On Sexuality

By watching our parents interact with one another we develop basic concepts of sexuality, intimacy and relationships in general. For those of us who are female, we learned how to be women by watching our mothers. We also learned about men by watching our fathers. For those who are male, lessons about being a man came from watching father, while information about females came from observing mother. Respect for our own sex develops as a result of how our same-sex parent felt about himself or herself. Respect for members of the opposite sex is developed by watching our same-sex parent relate to our opposite-sex parent.

Many of us leave our parents' home promising ourselves we will never involve ourselves in a relationship like THEIRS. But many of us, down the line, find that we too are in a dysfunctional relationship and ask how this could happen. Since our parents provide our first notion of what a relationship is, we usually end up doing one of two things in our own adult relationships. We become involved in relationships similar to those of our parents or we become involved with partners who appear to be opposite in character to our parents. Either extreme will prove dysfunctional.

Our parents' own sexuality and their beliefs and values about sex have a tremendous impact on us. Some of us are sexual abuse survivors without being aware of it. Some of the situations and experiences around issues of sexuality which took place in our homes while we were growing up are seen in society as normal. Human sexuality has lived in a closet of shame throughout history because of a lack of information. If we were sexually abused, we continue the cycle with our own children out of a lack of awareness. We are abusing our children because we don't know appropriate versus inappropriate behavior in regard to sexuality.

Lost Memories

There is a large population of individuals who have experienced severe sexual offenses but in order to survive as children, the experience or experiences have been repressed by the mind. As a result of this loss of memory, these adults are suffering the consequences of childhood sexual abuse but without the memory that would make sense of their suffering. Sexual addiction and eating disorders are but two of the many consequences of sexual abuse.

When a child is maltreated in any way by a parent, major caregiver or by a person in a position of authority, the impact can be lifelong. Children are naturally self-centered and narcissistic. They see the world as rotating around them, they believe they are the center of the universe. This perception of life is a normal and natural part of child development. Parents represent survival because children depend on them for food, clothing, shelter, nurturing and more. Because of this, children also see their parents as all-knowing and godlike. As a matter of fact, our first concept of a Higher Power or God comes from our perception of our parents. Our initial concept of a Higher Power usually has many of the characteristics our parents possess. It would be pretty scary for a child to know

Table 4.1. The Traumatic Memory Loss Process

Childhood	Adult

Conscious Awareness In The Here And Now

Sexual abuse experience with major caretaker during childhood → Feelings about being sexually abused

- Rage
- Physical pain
- Depression
- Grief
- Betrayal
- Shame

→ Memory loss → Feelings about the abusive experience which still remain even though the actual memory is not available in current conscious awareness

- Rage
- Physical pain
- Depression
- Grief
- Betrayal
- Shame

Unconscious Awareness Of Experiences In The Past

— Memory loss — sexual abuse experience with major caretaker during childhood
— Memory loss is a defense mechanism

Memory of traumatic childhood events, such as sexual abuse, are many times lost as a result of a need for safety. Since it is not safe to be aware that a major caretaker is inflicting pain as a result of abusive behavior, the experience moves to the unconscious. Even though the memory of the experience is not available in the conscious, the feelings associated with the abuse are still present.

all the imperfections that adults have because children depend on adults to be together enough to protect them and keep them safe.

For many of us who have not had healthy parenting, I believe addictions provide a type of dysfunctional parenting that we use to make up for the lack of childhood nurturing.

When a child is hurt emotionally, physically or sexually, it is due to the parents' inability to deal effectively with the adult world and not having the skills to provide healthy parenting. Abusive behavior by parents is also the resurfacing of their own unresolved abuse issues. Parents who are abusive tend to abuse their children in the same ways they were abused in their own childhood. To confuse matters even more, abusing parents also may not have memory recall of their own abuse and are often acting in ways they don't understand.

Self-Blame And Disassociation

Children live in a world of fantasy and magical thinking. This magical thinking provides a way for them to deal with the complexities in the world. With time, nurturing and maturity, children eventually grow up to be adults with the appropriate tools for dealing with the world as it really is. But when a parent or major caregiver is abusive, it is the child's magical thinking that allows him to survive the abuse. Since children see parents as powerful and all-knowing, it is not safe, for survival reasons, to see them as abusive or incompetent. When abuse occurs, a child will, with the help of self-centered, magical thinking, blame himself for the abuse. "I did something bad, so Daddy touched me there. It was my fault and I deserved to be hurt." The child will carry into and throughout adulthood a sense that "I am bad, unworthy." This feeling of unworthiness, inadequacy, incompleteness, emptiness is referred to as shame.

A child's sense of self is the product of those feelings reflected back to the child by the parents' behavior. If a child is mistreated by a parent, the message he receives is that he is bad, that if he were good, this abusive behavior from mother or father would not happen.

Children also "forget" hurtful incidents to remain as they *need* to see themselves, safe with those who have hurt them. This powerful defense mechanism has been called *disassociation, suppression* or *repression.* The mind is powerful and part of its job is to keep us safe and out of pain. If keeping us safe means forgetting, this is what the mind will do. If a father is sexually molesting his young daughter on a regular basis, the daughter, out of a need to survive emotionally and physically, may disassociate or forget the sexually abusive episodes. In this way, father can remain the "safe" parent she needs. It would not be safe to know that father is sexually out of control and regularly hurting her.

The Need To Learn Parenting

We know a lot about building space stations and exploring other planets in our solar system but in our world, most new parents do not know how to be parents. New parents are largely unprepared, with little, if any, information on child development so most will end up parenting in the only way they know, the way they themselves were parented.

When my son Aaron was born, Michael and I were at our wits' end as neither of us knew what was normal. I believed that every time Aaron cried, he was dying. I did not know that newborns cried at times just for the sake of crying. I would check his diaper, make sure he was not hungry, rock him and sometimes he would still cry! Finally, overwhelmed with fear that something must be terribly wrong, I took him to the pediatrician. Mind you, this off and on crying behavior is normal for babies but I thought happy, contented babies were always silent. I thought each time my baby cried It meant I was not parenting right. My pediatrician informed me as gently as she could that newborn babies sometimes just cry. Well, this was news to me! Michael and I had to seek help for healthy parenting and to this day, if we are unsure, we find someone who knows and ask for help. If I had not asked for help to understand newborn crying behavior, I could have done damage to my child out of ignorance, by trying to make him stop.

Unintentional Sexual Abuse By
Unenlightened Parents And Caregivers

Not knowing what is normal and age-appropriate can cause the average parent a lot of grief. I believe much child abuse happens because of this. So, exactly what is sexually abusive behavior? As I have said, many of us have been abused sexually and are unaware of it. We tend to view only sexual intercourse or penetration by an adult with a minor as sexual abuse. In reality, there are numerous ways in which children are sexually abused. The following is a list of behaviors which are considered by many therapists and helping professionals, including myself, to be sexually abusive acts against children. Many of these things happen in families due to lack of awareness. These are:

1. Not providing information about human sexuality.
2. Not providing information about puberty and sexual development, e.g., menstruation, sexual development in adolescence.
3. Not providing information about sexual values such as appropriate versus inappropriate behaviors.
4. Giving false information about sexuality — *If you masturbate, your penis will fall off. . . . Babies come from the cabbage patch . . . . Nice girls don't like sex. . . . Sex is dirty. . . . Sex is only for procreation . . .*
5. Giving too much information too soon, before the child is ready or able to understand it.
6. Denying bathroom or bedroom privacy.
7. Not providing positive, appropriate, healthy hugging and touching.
8. Being sexually repressed, never hugging or touching at all so that the child cannot imagine the parents having a sexual relationship.
9. Using God while shaming about sexual behavior — *God will punish you for masturbating . . . for having relationships with members of the opposite sex . . . for having sex before marriage.*

10. Excessive, sexual hugging and touching between parents in view of children.
11. Parental lack of modesty in dress, wearing of skimpy nightgowns, underwear — or nudity, once children are past toddler age.
12. Bathing with or being bathed by parents when children are past toddler age.
13. Leading a child to assume the same-sex parent role by being Daddy's Little Princess or Mama's Little Man or the role of surrogate spouse — also called emotional incest.
14. Enmeshing the child in adult sexual relationships or problems, specifically by discussing them with the child.
15. Using the child as a sexual shield between parents, for example by sleeping with the child when the child is past toddler age, providing an excuse for parents to avoid issues in their relationship.
16. Lack of sexual boundaries in the home, e.g., parents not locking the bedroom door while having sex when the children are at home, or forcing children to bathe together or sleep together when it is no longer comfortable for them.
17. Shaming children for being female or male — e.g., *You're stupid like all females, You're just like your father,* (when the father is dysfunctional).
18. Shaming the child for sexual physical development during puberty or otherwise, by inappropriate remarks about breast size, genitals and the like.
19. Calling a child sexually degrading names such as whore, slut, gigolo.
20. Shaming a child for having sexual feelings or ignoring the sexual feelings.
21. Not allowing dating relationships when age appropriate, overcontrolling dating relationships or not providing guidelines and structure for dating relationships.
22. Exposing children to arguments between parents around issues of sexuality or to witnessing sexual behavior between parents.
23. Excessive sexual joking and sexual remarks.
24. Exposing children to any type of pornography.

25. Parental extramarital sexual activities and affairs.
26. Sexual addiction, sexual acting out and escape through sexual fantasizing on the part of parents.
27. Excessive use of enemas.

Most parents are unaware of the impact of these behaviors on their children but in reality, these acts are inappropriate and sexually abusive. It is likely that these individuals had parents who also did the same things and they too were unaware of the impact.

Malicious Acts Of Child Sexual Abuse

The following are behaviors which are most commonly seen as sexually abusive and are usually intentional:

1. Voyeurism including covert and seductive glances, looks that are obviously sexual.
2. Touching or massaging in a sexual manner, sexualized backrubs or hand holding, bathing child in a sexual manner.
3. Sexualized hugging, touching inappropriately while hugging, hugging for too long or when the child doesn't want it and has no choice.
4. Seductive dancing, too closely, inappropriately, making the child feel trapped and without choice.
5. Lap sitting when it makes the child uncomfortable, inappropriate touching during lap sitting or when there is an erection or sexual stimulation on the part of the adult.
6. Wet or lingering kisses, kissing for too long or when the child feels uncomfortable.
7. Genital or breast touching or fondling.
8. Genital or breast tickling, sexual touching under the guise of play or roughhousing.
9. Sexualized rage, abuse or cruelty, making a child watch another be molested, raped or sexually abused or see one parent sexually abuse the other.
10. Sexual punishments, e.g., having to strip down or eat in the nude for not getting to the table on time, or to stand in the nude.

11. Forcing children to be sexual with one another, sexualized games or play.
12. Exposure to masturbation either on the child by an adult or by forcing the child to masturbate an adult.
13. Penetration, genitally or orally, with finger, objects or sexual organs, i.e., oral sex, anal sex or intercourse.
14. Exposure to "weird" sex, sexual torture or rape.
15. Exposure to or being used in sexual activities in cult situations, such as in satanic worshipping or black magic practices.

Whenever a touch feels uncomfortable or wrong to a child, it usually is an inappropriate touch — probably abusive. Children suffer serious consequences from sexual abuse. Many remain untreated due to memory loss, the most frustrating consequence because the loss usually involves big blocks of time throughout childhood. These individuals may have totally lost memory recall of those ages during which the sexual abuse was occurring. Without the history of the abuse, it is difficult, if not impossible, to understand certain feelings that the individual may be having. Many helping professionals, without an understanding of sexual abuse relative to memory loss, end up only treating the symptoms of the sexual abuse, never knowing that it is the real issue. I heard a therapist once say to a client that since she didn't have concrete memory of her sexual abuse, it never really happened. Eventually, after appropriate therapy, this same client remembered an incident of sexual abuse.

I believe a Higher Spiritual Power provides us with escape mechanisms from childhood abusive situations. Memory loss can be achieved by detaching from the physical self emotionally in order not to feel the abuse as it happens. Some individuals I have worked with have reported out-of-body experiences during abusive situations. An out-of-body experience is similar to what is called a near-death experience. During close calls with death many individuals have reported leaving their bodies. During such experiences these individuals are aware of their surroundings and can hear people talking, while they float above their bodies. This may sound farfetched to some but Raymond Moody, M.D., has documented many accounts of near-death experiences by individuals while they were being operated on. Reports from these individuals state consistently that they left their physical body and were aware of all that was happening during the operation such as conversation, operating procedures and even what the operating room looked like. They have reported back to their doctors what was said while they supposedly were under anesthesia. Near-death experiences have also been documented in other traumatic situations such as car wrecks. For more information on near-death experiences, look for Raymond Moody's first work on this subject titled *Life After Life*.

Aftermath Of Childhood Sexual Trauma

For individuals who experienced traumatic sexual abuse during childhood, leaving the physical body emotionally — or, in some cases, physically — is a safety mechanism for protecting the fragile make-up of a child. But, even though the memory of the experience retreats underground into the unconscious, the feelings — both emotional and, in many cases, physical — remain. Some of the physical feelings which may resurface from time to time as illness in the body are . . . allergies; asthma; rashes; muscle tremors and body tics; genital, pelvic or abdominal pains; vaginal or urethral discharge; bladder or urinary tract infections, usually starting at an early age.

I have worked with many incest and sexual abuse survivors who initially came to therapy due to some psychological difficulty related to sexual abuse. Sadly though, many of them had previously seen other helping professionals who had little knowledge about sexual abuse.

Sleep Disorders

For some survivors, a consequence of their abuse is *sleep disorders*. For those who were customarily molested at night, sleep was not a time of safety. Some report that they had the most difficulty sleeping during those hours of the night when, in childhood, they were abused. Some victims also wake up on a regular basis in the middle of the night, feeling startled and anxious. This night-time *startle response* is associated with the hour at which the trauma took place originally. It is in response to *feeling memories.* When individuals do not have memory recall of their abuse and seek professional help, most professionals who do not understand abuse issues either prescribe sleep medication or refer them to someone else who also prescribes sleep medication and the patient is set up for another potential problem — prescription drug addiction.

Some individuals who have been sexually abused also experience frightening dreams and fantasies which make the prospect of going to sleep an unpleasant one. I have worked with several such children who feared going to sleep at night. Some of them sleep with their parents on a regular basis, because they fear being alone in their own room. The main complaint is always around not feeling safe. When asked what it is they are afraid of the response is always monsters, vampires, robbers and, in one instance, a horror movie personality called Freddy Krueger. Other fears involve snakes under the bed, spiders on the floor or, as one child put it, "crawly things on the walls." Some childhood nightmares are normal, but when the fears are overwhelming, they are sleep disorders and there is an underlying unease. Children, with the help of magical thinking, will turn the sexual abuser into a personality that is less frightening. Their need for survival requires their major caregivers to be "safe." If a child is being molested by a major caregiver, he or she will project the abusive behavior into a fantasy fear in order to keep their safe caretaker — so instead of fearing mother, father, grandparents, siblings or whoever is violating them, the fear will focus on monsters, vampires, robbers, ghosts, even Freddy Krueger. Children who suffer from these difficulties grow up to be adults who fear things that "go bump in the night." Some adult sexual abuse survivors sleep with many pillows or blankets in response to a need for safety. They need to sleep with night lights on or they may need to keep closet or bathroom lights on throughout the night. In some cases they need a glass or two of wine or other alcoholic beverage to get to sleep and curb night-time nerves. For those who medicate to get to sleep at night, the consequences can be progressive alcoholism or drug dependency.

Phobias

Another consequence of childhood sexual abuse can be *phobias.* A phobia is an excessive, overwhelming fear such as of snakes, spiders or things that go bump in the night. Some sexual abuse survivors also are excessively afraid of blood, shots, doctors, dentists, pain or being touched by members of the same or the opposite sex. For children at the start of the sexual abuse, there may be an onset of fear of school, crowds or open spaces. Grades may drop and illnesses may develop in response to traumatic abuse. Fear of crowds and open spaces, referred to as agoraphobia, may develop. Unfortunately, many helping professionals treat this disorder with prescription drugs, never addressing the underlying issues, maintaining that all phobic or panic behavior is chemically related. Panic attacks, for some sexual abuse survivors, can cause incapacitating feelings of confusion and fear. These appear to take place during times of frustration or of feeling trapped and out of control. As a result of overwhelming fears and phobias, sufferers may isolate, cutting themselves off, at times, from the outside world. Helping professionals who do not understand the consequences of sexual abuse, have diagnosed behaviors such as these as borderline personality disorders, neurotic disorders and, in some cases, psychosis. Some abuse survivors have wound up in psychiatric hospitals or lock-up wards under the guise of having a "nervous breakdown." In these situations, the symptoms are treated while the underlying issues of sexual abuse are rarely addressed.

When a child is molested, the nonverbal message he or she receives is, "You do not have any choice. You are unworthy." Most victims talk about feelings of depression that hit them from out of the blue. A feeling of incompleteness and emptiness comes from time to time. This can be so overwhelming that life seems to have no meaning. Since they come from dysfunctional families, they also have grown up with the belief that it is not all right to talk about what is going on. As a result, they do not have the coping skills to process depression and grief. Finally, because of the dysfunction within the family system and as a result of the abuse trauma, they have difficulty not only in trusting themselves but in trusting others as well.

When family system dysfunction is combined with issues of severe abuse, the results can be lethal. I have worked with a number of sexual abuse survivors who, at some point in their lives, felt that life had absolutely no meaning. Many of them have not been able to trust enough at those times to talk about their feelings with anyone. Some who tried were given psychiatric labels and drugs. The hopelessness can lead survivors in a couple of directions.

Suicide

For some, *suicide* seems a viable option. Most of the sexual abuse survivors I have worked with have contemplated suicide at least once and some have followed through with attempts to end their lives.

Addictions

Another option for coping with pain is *addiction.* Addiction, which in my opinion is a slow form of suicide, can be a way of temporarily covering up the feelings of despair. The relief that addiction brings for abuse victims has a lifesaving purpose for a while but eventually it backfires.

I do not think people decide to become addicts. I believe the decision is made for them by genetic factors, family of origin history and childhood abuse issues. Alcohol, food, drugs, sex, work, religion can become temporary "cures" for those of us who lack the necessary coping skills for living in the adult world. For sexual abuse survivors, excessive or addictive use of alcohol or drugs can provide escape from the overwhelming feelings that make life so painful. Many survivors have been raised in alcoholic homes and are genetically predisposed to the disease of alcoholism or to drug addiction, which temporarily cushion the realities of life.

For more information on the disease of alcoholism and drug addiction, contact your local Regional Drug and Alcohol

Council or Alcoholics Anonymous. It is impossible to address the issues of sexual abuse or family of origin as long as feelings are being masked with drugs or alcohol.

Eating Disorders

Another consequence of sexual abuse is eating disorders. To this day, I have not met one sexual abuse survivor who does not have some sort of eating disorder. There are many kinds of eating disorders but for our purposes we will be discussing only a few of them briefly.

For those interested in a more in-depth discussion of eating disorders, refer to my book, *Eat Like A Lady: Guide For Overcoming Bulimia* (Health Communications, 1989) for more information.

Obsessive-compulsive eaters are usually 20 pounds or more overweight and use food to medicate their feelings the same way that alcoholics use alcohol. For many obsessive-compulsive eaters, the added weight is a wall of safety that keeps them from experiencing who they really are. It's as if the weight is a mechanism to keep the abusers away. Obsessive-compulsive eaters are addicted to food because it provides the nurturing and comfort that wasn't available in the family of origin. For those obsessive-compulsive eaters who are sexual abuse survivors, the added weight is also a way of withdrawing from the unsafe outside world. By isolating and receiving comfort from food, it becomes unnecessary to risk close contact with others.

Many obsessive-compulsive eaters gained weight shortly after or during a period of sexual abuse, unconsciously hoping the wall of weight would keep them safe. But, as with all solid walls, little comes through them and rarely does anything move out from behind them. It's like being enclosed in a cylinder, fearing what's outside. The sad thing about this is that even though obsessive-compulsive eaters may derive a false sense of security from food, the pain, rage — and in some cases, the memories — needed for healing do not find their way out. Many of the wonderful growth opportunities in life never make their way through until the eating disorder is addressed and recovery from food addiction is achieved.

Family of origin and abuse issues must be dealt with for healing to take place.

Still another eating disorder which appears to be a result of sexual abuse is *bulimia*. Bulimia involves binging on large amounts of food, be it heads of lettuce or boxes of cookies, and then purging to rid the body of the calories by vomiting, by using laxatives, by fasting, excessive exercise or other means. Most bulimics are weight appropriate and have an appearance of self-confidence but this appearance is false. Prior to recovery as a bulimic, I had a real need to be in control and appeared very together. The false outer look of security covered feelings of pain, fear, rage, loneliness and shame that I carried inside.

Bulimics avoid the realities of life by altering painful feelings with binging on food. Binging becomes a temporary problem-solver. Purging is also mood-altering and there is an obsession with not gaining much weight and with being out of control. For sexual abuse survivors who are bulimic, the belief is, "If I appear perfect and in control on the outside, maybe my inside feelings of pain and shame will be under control and go away." Initially, the function of the binging behavior is to cover up the shame but it only accomplishes this temporarily. Eventually, the binging behavior adds more shame to the shame that was already there and there is a need to purge this feeling away. Purging seems to be a symbolic way of ridding the sexual abuse survivor of the shame associated with being severely violated as a child. Though bulimia can be a temporary solution, as with all addictions, it eventually backfires. Because the obsession with food and purging is so great, this addiction also becomes a distraction from the unresolved sexual abuse issues. If there is a memory loss of the abuse experience, bulimia pushes the memory down further into the unconscious, preventing any chance of healing.

Anorexia Nervosa is another eating disorder that can create a temporary distraction for sexual abuse survivors. Anorexia Nervosa involves a 25 percent body weight loss during which the sufferer believes nothing is wrong. Anorexics suffer from intense delusional thinking about their physical appearance, and in many cases continue to believe they are overweight when in reality they are emaciated. There is a chemical imbalance in the body because of malnutrition. As a result, the mood is altered and anorexics tend to suffer from a hyperactive condition I call an anorexic high. The need for perfection and control is all encompassing and many have close brushes with death because of the intense denial associated with this eating disorder.

I recently confronted an anorexic about her weight loss. She looked me directly in the eye and said she appreciated my concern but her eating was not her problem. As I have said, sexual abuse survivors have strong feelings of unworthiness and incompleteness. They feel violated and damaged. What better way to avoid confronting the pain of sexual abuse than to become totally obsessed with achieving perfection. Anorexics work toward perfecting their bodies and eventually the obsession turns to delusional addiction. Delusion of what one's body really looks like also contributes to an inaccurate perception of life in general. Many anorexics are misdiagnosed as psychotic or borderline, when in reality they suffer from addiction. The need to escape the realities of life and see the world as perfect indicates a strong need for safety. The unconscious belief is, "I can be safe in a perfect world." By not seeing life as it really is, with all of its facets, the illusionary fantasy of the anorexic continues to push away the painful truth about family dysfunction and childhood abuse.

Individuals suffering from traumatic childhood sexual abuse carry with them into adulthood the scars of their experiences. Eating disorders, like all addictions, are but symptoms and cover for the pain that lives deep within. Preoccupation with weight gains and losses are distractions from much larger issues and these behaviors temporarily prevent the characteristic pain, shame, rage, loneliness and grief from surfacing. These feelings need to be felt to attain a healthy recovery from family of origin trauma. Also, these addictions discourage healthy communication with self and others and true intimacy is almost impossible to achieve. Because sexual abuse survivors who have eating disorders have a number of unresolved issues, chances for healthy relationships are slim.

5

Sexual Abuse: Impact On Intimacy

We know that our first concepts of relationships come when we are children, observing our caregivers interacting with one another. We also learn through our experiences with others during childhood. On an unconscious level, we develop rules and ideas about relationships from these early experiences. Since our first model of a relationship is usually our parents, who are seen as all-knowing, we therefore believe their relationship is the way relationships are. If there is sexual acting out going on in our family of origin, we believe this, too, is the way things are supposed to be, otherwise it would stop. The following story describes the consequences of childhood sexual abuse in the adult life of a survivor.

Jean's Story

Jean's family of origin appeared perfect. Growing up, all her neighborhood friends envied her relationship with her parents. For many years Jean believed her relationship with her parents was perfect and that she had grown up in a typical family. Her father worked very hard and was always at the office. Though she often missed him her mother reminded her regularly that if it weren't for her father's work, they wouldn't live in such a nice house. Jean's mother said it was selfish to be upset with her father for not being home more often, after all he was doing for her by working hard to make money. Jean felt very guilty after these discussions with her mother and eventually learned not to bring up the subject. When Jean's father was home, she was very happy and loved to spend as much time as she could with him. Sometimes Jean would sit on her father's lap and watch television with him. Though she enjoyed sitting on his lap, on several occasions her father touched her on her private parts. When he did this, she felt very uncomfortable and at times his touching her in this area of her body hurt a little. But Jean didn't want to say anything because she was afraid her father would get mad and never spend time with her again. So Jean decided to just ignore this by blocking it out as if it were not happening. She learned how to block it out so well that she completely forgot about it when it happened.

Everyone always said Jean's mother was a good church-going woman who put her family first. Jean thought her mother was a bit gruff but thought her mother needed to be this way to keep the family running smoothly. Jean got the feeling her mother was happiest when her father was at work and she did not see them hug one another very often. She wondered if they really liked each other. Once she heard them fighting late at night but it wasn't clear what they were fighting about. She remembers hearing her mother say something about another woman but didn't understand what that meant.

As Jean grew up, she became a bit overweight. Her mother told her that if she didn't lose weight, people would not like her and she'd never have a boyfriend. Jean didn't understand why she liked to eat so much but thought her mother must be right and resolved to follow the diet her mother had developed for her. Though she tried, she found herself sneaking snacks between meals. Her mother eventually discovered this and accused her of being weak-willed and lazy.

Eventually, Jean went off to college, excited about the adventure that living away from home would bring. She missed her father but was grateful, in a way, to get some distance from her mother. In one of her classes, she met George and was very attracted to him. He was a hard worker and made exceptional grades. Jean was impressed with him and dieted to please him. He said he liked her the way she was but that she could stand to lose a few pounds. He also suggested she change her hairstyle and several times he went shopping with her and picked out the clothes he thought would be appropriate for her. Jean was overwhelmed with all the attention George gave her.

Eventually they began having a sexual relationship. Jean really didn't care for sex very much and learned to block out the experience while she had sex with George. Jean believed she was in a perfect relationship and was happier than she had ever been until one day a girlfriend shared some unpleasant news with her. She told Jean that she had seen George out with other women on a number of occasions and felt she had to tell her. Jean was angry with her friend for "telling such awful lies" and said George would never do such a thing. She believed the accusations were so ridiculous that she didn't even bother to bring them up to George. But one day when she was out to lunch with a girlfriend, she spotted George and another woman in a corner booth, caressing one another. Jean ended the relationship there and then and told herself she would never be hurt like that again.

George's parents were both alcoholic. He knew they both had affairs and he never understood why they stayed together. He was attracted to Jean's innocence and really cared for her but felt he needed sex from more than one source in order to be satisfied. He was confused when Jean cut off their relationship because, as he saw it, his relationship with the other women was only physical. In reality, George was addicted to sex, just as Jean's father was. His idea of a relationship was modeled on his parents, both of whom were sexually addicted and dysfunctional.

For a year or so, Jean avoided involvements with men — until the evening she met Paul at a party. Paul seemed gentle and quiet and Jean found he was easy to talk to. Paul asked for her phone number and several months later Jean was in another relationship. Paul was very attentive and she enjoyed his company. He seemed dedicated to his job and appeared to have a stable income. Eventually Paul and Jean married and lived happily for several years after. They rarely disagreed and seemed content with one another. Jean still was not comfortable with sex but continued to tune out while making love. Paul seemed to be the perfect husband and Jean believed she had nothing to complain about although she did resent the pornographic magazines she found from time to time. She thought this must be normal for men. She noticed that Paul kept them in the bathroom and wondered why. Ultimately, she concluded that it was none of her business and ignored it.

Over the years, Jean and Paul had sex less and less and she thought she must be doing something wrong. When they did have sex, it was purely physical with no emotional involvement, as though Paul was somewhere else emotionally. She felt hurt and unloved and also noticed that she was eating to comfort herself for the pain in her relationship with Paul. Slowly she began to put on weight.

As Jean put on more weight, Paul found her more unattractive and sexually unappealing. She was beginning to remind him of his mother and he was spending more time at the office, to avoid contact with her. He learned he could take care of his sexual needs by masturbating and he slowly pulled away from Jean more and more. As he did, Jean felt more hurt and turned to food for comfort even more. In time, Paul and Jean became strangers to one another, though they continued the relationship for the sake of convenience.

Jean's difficulty with relationships stemmed from her relationship with her father, even though it appeared that the men in her adult life were the problem. Her first experience with a member of the opposite sex was with her father, a workaholic who used his work as an excuse to avoid intimate contact with her mother. He, too, was a sexual abuse survivor but had no memory of those incidents in his childhood when his mother, herself having been molested by an uncle, fondled him while bathing him. When Jean's father molested her by fondling her vagina while they watched television, he told himself this really wasn't wrong and he covered his shame by working very hard at his job. He really loved his daughter and did his best to provide for her and make her happy.

Jean's mother had a lot of hostility toward men in general, resulting from being sexually abused when *she* was a child. She knew that her husband periodically had affairs but decided just to ignore it, hoping that if she did so, the affairs would stop.

Though Jean blocked the experiences with her father out of her memory, she still felt she was bad. She found, though, that food could make her feel less unworthy. In reality, her father's behavior was shameless since he was having his sexual needs taken care of by abusing his daughter. Even though she "lost" the experiences, the message she was unconsciously receiving was that she must be bad or her father wouldn't hurt her this way. Jean was very needy for her father's attention and fear of abandonment contributed to her blocking out his actions. Her mother, always somewhat jealous of the relationship between her husband and her daughter, never said anything for fear he would abandon her by having affairs. Instead she tried to be the perfect wife and mother by keeping things running smoothly.

Paul's Story

Paul initially appeared to be a stable individual who would remain faithful. But Paul did not have to go outside of his marriage to have an affair. Paul had fantasy affairs with the women in his pornographic magazines. In Paul's family, the father spent most of his time at his office and the mother was chronically sick and took a lot of prescription drugs. Paul didn't know why his mother was always sick but he felt it was his job to *not* upset her.

Paul had a baby-sitter who spent a great deal of time with him because of his mother's illnesses. The baby-sitter, an attractive young woman, would occasionally take a shower with him and at these times she would fondle his penis. He never told his mother about it because he didn't want to upset her. He didn't think about sharing it with his father because his father was never home anyway. Paul remembers the experience of showering with his baby-sitter as being pleasurable but at the same time something about it felt wrong. As an adult, Paul laughs off these experiences, claiming they were not damaging. He believes that, if anything, the incidents with the baby-sitter taught him something.

Paul's experiences with the baby-sitter were sexually abusive because he did not have a choice in the matter. The baby-sitter was using her position of authority to get her sexual needs taken care of. Paul's best interests were not being served. These encounters set Paul up for adult relationships based purely on sexual gratification. He also learned that he could deal with his feelings of aloneness by masturbating. When he faced disappointment with Jean, he quickly learned that he could avoid dealing with her by retreating into his fantasy relationships. His fantasy relationships were more satisfying than his relationship with Jean. Paul is a sex addict who used his addiction to avoid intimacy with his wife. Also, since Paul did not deal with his feelings in a healthy way, they were never resolved.

Jean felt shame about Paul's lack of attention. Since he avoided his feelings with addiction, Jean felt them for him. (Have you ever stood next to someone who is angry about something but not addressing it and then felt confused when they denied being angry only to walk away feeling angry yourself? This process also happens with other feelings.) Paul carried a lot of shame from his unresolved family of origin issues. He avoided dealing with this by acting out sexually with fantasy. Jean felt his shame and believed she felt ashamed because she was an inadequate person and wife. She hid these feelings of shame by eating. When she did so, she was being irresponsible by not working them through in an adult manner. She was using childhood survival skills to cope as she did in her original family and to avoid holding Paul responsible for his inappropriate sexually addictive behavior.

As she continued to eat addictively, masking her shame with food, Paul began to feel the shame she was not being responsible for in regard to her addiction. The shame he felt became overwhelming and he in turn covered it up by acting out with compulsive masturbating instead of confronting the dysfunction within the relationship. And so the cycles of addictive behavior continued, making any chance for true intimacy impossible. For Jean, Paul became her focus, distracting her from her own family of origin issues and addictive behavior. For Paul, Jean became his focus, keeping him from addressing his family of origin issues and addictive behavior. Both were caught in a common cycle which continues the dysfunction from one generation to another. Paul felt that if Jean would just lose weight, the problems in the relationship would be solved. Jean felt that if Paul would just love her the way she needs to be loved, their relationship would be perfect. Neither realized that they both needed to heal themselves from within before they could experience real intimacy in the relationship.

6

Sexual Abuse:
Prelude To Sexual Addiction

As we grow up in our families, we develop certain ideas regarding sex. We carry these learned beliefs into adult life and to a degree we pass them on to our children. Our beliefs about appropriate sexual behavior versus what is inappropriate may be based on the beliefs of our great-grandparents or even our great-great-grandparents. What is so confusing about this is that usually we tell ourselves we will be more progressive and open than our predecessors with regard to matters of sexuality, only to find ourselves later on repeating some of the family traditions that we saw our parents practice.

While working with sexually abusive and sexually addictive family systems, it was noted that these dysfunctions have been active for generations. Those individuals who are sexual abusers are also sexual addicts who have been sexually abused themselves.

Children develop physically, psychologically and socially through a number of stages as they grow into adulthood. Along with physical, psychological and social development, sexual development is an important part of the growth process. Many dedicated individuals throughout the latter part of the last century have explored the stages of development that children go through as they move toward adulthood. For those of us from dysfunctional families, our awareness of these stages may be very limited. I had to begin investigating what the stages of the child development process were when I had my own son. Even as a professional in the helping field I had little awareness of what behaviors were appropriate for certain ages. Most of us from dysfunctional homes grew up with parents who, as a result of their upbringing, did not understand the developmental process.

Today, many of us have unrealistic expectations of our children because of a lack of knowledge. Those interested in more information about child development should refer to *The Psychology of the Child,* by Jean Piaget (1969) or *Montessori: A Modern Approach* by Paula Polk Lillard (1972). For our purposes we will only be exploring the sexual development of children as it is related to sexual abuse and sexually addictive behavior. Our discussion on this process will be limited because in-depth exploration would require a separate writing.

In early childhood, from toddler age to pre-puberty or pre-adolescence, children progress through a number of developmental stages which are focused on self-discovery and exploration of the world around them. They see the world as revolving around them. Their concept of what the world is like originates from what they observe as their parents and other adults interact within the family system. The naturally self-centered child depends on those adults for every need. They depend on the major caregivers for affirmation of their feelings and perceptions of the world around them. If mother and father fight and it is not explained to the child that the fighting is not about him, the self-centered child will believe that he caused the fight. If mother and father divorce and it is not explained to the child that he or she is not responsible and is still loved by both parents, the self-centered child will believe he caused the separation. I have worked with many children from severely dysfunctional homes and they all believed that somehow they were the cause of the dysfunction. Usually the parents of those children did not know that their children felt responsible for the adults' problems.

Sexually, during this phase of development, children begin to explore their bodies. When my son turned two, we began toilet training. Previous to this he had discovered that he had a penis. During toilet training he found it amazing that his urine came from his penis. He saw that as not only exciting but magical to a degree. Children begin to learn how their bodies work through exploration. Eventually, they also begin to learn that their genitals can bring them pleasure and for a while this is a source of focus and excitement. Eventually, other things within the world they live in become more important and their attention turns elsewhere.

If children are sexually abused during this time of growth, the sexual developmental process may come to a halt. As I mentioned earlier, our first concept of a Higher Power or God comes from our parents and major caregivers. Because adults are physically bigger and responsible for meeting all of a child's needs, he sees them as God-like. This is a normal part of the child's development. Because the perception is one of authority and of being God-like, children believe adults are always right. The fear of being abandoned, left alone in the world, also perpetuates this belief and consequently loyalty ties are strong even when adult behaviors are abusive. Children need to believe their parents and caregivers are right because their survival depends on this. A young child would not feel safe knowing his parents are fallible. It would be very scary to know that his parents don't know what they are doing. When parents and major caregivers sexually abuse a child, that young, needy child cannot see the abuser as being wrong. What the child does believe is that in some way he is responsible, that he was in the wrong.

This belief is then carried into adulthood, causing dysfunction and pain in relationships with others and self. There is a feeling of incompleteness, emptiness and unworthiness. When a parent or major caregiver sexually abuses a child, his behavior is irresponsible and shameless, he or she is using the child to fill his own adult needs. The interests of the child are not considered and the position of authority is misused. As mentioned earlier, the mind of a young child does its best to protect that child and in many cases, memory of the experience moves to the unconscious. Though the memory may not be available, the feelings of unworthiness remain, along with a sense of emptiness. Also a bond based on sexual abuse is formed with the abuser. On an unconscious level, the child believes that if he or she were not bad, this would not happen. So, the child begins to work for approval from the abuser, hoping that if he is good enough, he will not be hurt again. This abuse bond is carried into adulthood where relationships are with individuals who are like the original abuser.

As adults, these children find relationships with abusive individuals and believe they do not have the choice of saying *no* to emotional, sexual or physical abuse. They believe that in some way they deserve it. Since childhood is a time of physical exploration, sexual abuse at this time can halt sexual development and the child can become stuck emotionally. Because of the abuser's perceived power, the child believes that this must be the way things are supposed to be. The abusive experience, because of this belief, follows the child into adulthood and affects adult sexual relationships. If the child is stuck in the physical phase of the sexual development process, mature intimacy in adulthood will be difficult, if not impossible.

Now let's explore how sexual abuse during this phase of child development can set the stage for sexual addiction later. The following scenario may give us some understanding of this process.

Early Childhood

When George was four years old, he had a baby-sitter, Sue, who sat with him regularly when his parents went out on Saturday nights. Sue was 14 years old. Her father was alcoholic and sexually addicted. He would drink regularly at the bars until closing time, around two in the morning. For many years when Sue was younger, after her father came home from a night of drinking, he would crawl into bed with her and fondle her genitals. As she grew to adolescence he stopped coming to her room late at night and at times Sue thought he didn't like her anymore. She knew something didn't feel right when her father came into her bed, but during that period, it was the only time she had any kind of physical touch from her father. When she reached adolescence, she felt rejected and abandoned by him. In reality, as Sue matured her father was no longer interested in her sexually. He felt safe while she was younger because he knew he had power over her and she was not as threatening as an adult would be. Sue's father is incapable of having a mature relationship with an adult woman.

Sue's mother was always angry and jealous of the relationship between Sue and her father. Sometimes Sue feels guilty, as if she were the cause of the difficulty between her parents. Her mother was very critical of her and Sue felt as though she could never please her.

While babysitting for George, she would give him a bath before putting him to bed and while bathing him, she would play with his penis until he had an erection. Sue didn't see anything wrong with this since George seemed to like it, too. George did like it but then thought something must be wrong when Sue told him never to tell anyone. Sue was doing to George what had been done to her by her father. This behavior between George and Sue continued for about a year.

At 16, Sue became pregnant and disappeared for a while. Her father was outraged and her mother accused her of being a whore. Sue's first concept of what a relationship with a male was about came from her relationship with her father. She had learned from this relationship with her father that having sex with someone was love. When her father rejected her, she sought out sex with others in an attempt to fill up the feelings of unworthiness and emptiness. As a result, she became pregnant. Having sex, for Sue, meant receiving love. Sex covered up her emptiness and loneliness. After having the baby, Sue has had a series of relationships with alcoholic and sexually addicted men. She believes that as long as she is having good sex, her relationships are solid. Sue is a sex addict in that she uses sex to camouflage her feelings of unworthiness, lone-liness, sadness, fear and inadequacy.

When her relationships fall apart, she feels totally responsi-ble and wonders what she did wrong, just as she did when her father rejected her. When she feels rejected, she starts to binge on large quantities of food, trying to mask the shame she feels within. She is also bulimic and engages in that eating behavior when she doesn't have a man in her life. At times she feels that mother was right, that she really is a whore but in reality, what she is feeling is the shame of being sexually abused — by her father, physically — by her mother, verbally. Sue is scared to live and afraid to die. She is trapped in the shame of addiction.

At six, George begins to act out sexually with other children in the neighborhood. Young children are naturally curious about sexuality and normal sexual exploration usually in-volves looking — "I'll show you mine if you show me yours" — and sometimes touching, usually followed by "That is gross!" If acting out sexually between children becomes more involved than that, the possibility of previous sexual abuse is high. For George, sexual acting out with other children involved excessive inappropriate touching of others' genitals. George also masturbates a lot because it makes him feel good. His mother tells him he is a bad boy and that his penis is dirty. When she catches him masturbating, she makes him stand in a corner. Children who develop normally during this stage of growth eventually discover that their genitals bring them pleasure. Off and on there is focus on the area of the genitals. But when a child knows exactly where to touch and how to touch and does so excessively, this may also be an indicator of possible sexual abuse. When George's mother shames him, he feels that something is very wrong with him, that he must *be* bad because his mother *says* he is bad. He doesn't understand how something that feels so good can be so bad. He decides his mother must be right and that some-thing is wrong with him — possibly his body.

In reality, George's mother was sexually abused by her grandfather when she was four years old but she does not have memory recall of the experience. She dislikes sex, seeing it as dirty, and is hostile toward men. She believes men are not to be trusted. She tells her son, George, that he is just like his father. George continues to masturbate but still feels bad about it once in a while. He masturbates when he feels sad or angry and is careful that his mother does not catch him.

George's father is rarely home because he is a workaholic and is always at work. George wishes he could spend more time with his father and often wonders if he has done something bad to keep his father away so much. When his father is not at work, he is out playing golf. George hates golf because he feels it takes his father away from him. He thinks that his father loves golf more than him. Once he said something to his mother about the amount of time his father spent on the golf course. His mother accused him of selfishly begrudging his father the relaxation time. George never brought it up again.

Adolescence

When he is about 12 years old, George discovers some magazines with pictures of nude women in his father's nightstand drawer. George is amazed at the number of magazines his father has and wonders how long he has had them. While looking through one of the magazines George begins to have an erection, so he takes the magazine to the bathroom and masturbates.

At puberty, adolescents begin to notice members of the opposite sex. As hormonal changes occur and physical maturity begins, sex and sexuality are once again a major focus. Relationships with others become an important part of adolescence along with an almost obsessive concern for physical appearance. Fantasy plays an important part during this stage of development and discussion usually involves body shape of females by males and preoccupation with physical attractiveness on the part of the females. Dating relationships begin and sexual activity usually is kissing and light touching. For adolescents, members of the opposite sex bring magic and excitement to their lives for the first time. Their bodies are reacting in ways that are very new and at times scary. There is a great deal of fear during adolescence. The fear usually concerns not being liked or accepted. Social skills are awkward and there are intense feelings of inadequacy. Fantasy usually is about a relationship with a perfect partner. Part of the fantasy is that this perfect partner will be a reflection of who the adolescent is and make him or her complete. If the opposite-sex parent treats the adolescent with respect, he will progress through the awkward stage of learning to relate to members of the opposite sex.

If the opposite-sex or same-sex parent is addicted, has unresolved family of origin issues or allows himself or herself to be abused and degraded in any way, our model of how to treat members of the opposite sex and same sex will be tainted. For example, if, as children, we grow up with a father who is a workaholic and never available, as George did, we will grow up believing that all men should be/are unavailable because we never had our need for attention fulfilled by a father. Women will be attracted to men with characteristics similar to their father's. Something about these men will feel familiar and comfortable. But when these women try to get their need for attention fulfilled by the men, they will be sadly disappointed.

For those of us who grew up with a mother like George's, our relationships with women, in adulthood, will be dysfunctional. Living with a mother who has a lot of unresolved hostility can set us up to have relationships as adults with women who have a great deal of unresolved anger. If mother was angry as a result of her own family of origin abuse and never addressed it, her children will believe they are the cause of her anger. The naturally self-centered child believes that when adults are angry or sad it is because of something they have done. Also, in many cases, adults with a great deal of unresolved anger misdirect their anger away from their own abuse issues and blame their feelings on their children. Several clients I have worked with who were sexual abuse survivors had difficulty directing their anger toward those who abused them. Instead, they would rage at their own children, verbally and in some cases physically, and had unrealistic expectations of them. As they worked through their abuse issues they were able to lower their expectations of their children and allow them to be age appropriate.

Since George grew up in a home with an unavailable father and a hostile mother, masturbation became a way to nurture himself. He had learned that his parents were not safe and so he developed a specific set of survival skills to allow him to survive in his dysfunctional family. I have worked with sexual abuse survivors who used masturbation during childhood as a way to nurture themselves. Most of them sensed that it was compulsive, that there was something not normal about how often they masturbated. This behavior is, for many, the prelude to sexual addiction.

George was interested in girls at his school but never felt secure enough to approach them and talk with them. At times he would masturbate while fantasizing about them but he rarely felt comfortable enough to risk approaching them. When he fantasized about them he was safe and in control and he never had to worry about being rejected or hurt. Because of his dysfunctional relationship with his mother, George felt very insecure with members of the opposite sex. Since his father was unavailable, George did not have a male model to observe and learn from.

Adulthood

As he matured, George did begin having relationships with more females. He slowly developed skills for communicating with them by observing his friends at school. He still masturbated quite frequently and kept an extensive pornography collection in his closet.

His first girlfriend, Jill, came from an extremely dysfunctional family. Her father was an alcoholic, the life of the party when he drank. He wasn't verbally abusive like some drinkers George had known. When George was at Jill's house, her father always offered him a beer and seemed like a very friendly guy, but George felt uncomfortable with the way Jill's father treated her. He noticed that Jill was her father's Little Princess and he felt uneasy when she would sit on her father's lap — at 18 years of age. George felt that Jill's relationship with

her father was more than the typical father-daughter relationship. He said something to her about it once and Jill became
angry with him for talking about her father in that way. She
said he didn't know how wonderful her father really was.

George also noticed that Jill was obsessed with her weight
and physical appearance. She was constantly dieting and ex-
ercising. She even jokingly said that when she felt too full,
she would just throw up. George thought this was unusual
but decided not to say anything for fear of her anger. He felt
awful when Jill got angry, even if her anger wasn't directed at
him. He was afraid to tell her how he really felt about her
family for fear she would leave him. He had learned how to
keep his feelings to himself in his own family and he did the
same with Jill.

Eventually Jill broke off her relationship with George. He
could not figure out what he had done to cause her to end
the relationship. In reality, Jill found someone she considered
more attractive and told George he was not meeting her
needs. Jill was an incest survivor and a bulimic. She was also
an adult child of an alcoholic. Her father had abused her
sexually when she was very young but she didn't have memory recall of the incident. During her teenage years she and
her father had an emotionally incestuous relationship and she
was his surrogate spouse. Jill carried around a lot of anger
because of the incest and misdirected it toward those male
friends whom she dated. She would only go out with males
who could give her something, such as school prestige or
popularity. She was destined to continue this behavior into
adulthood, having relationships only with men who would
provide for her materially. She enjoyed sex for the sake of
having someone hug her and at times participated in degrading sexual activity in order to keep a relationship going. She
disguised the shame she felt after such sexual episodes by
binging on large quantities of food and then throwing up. Jill
didn't know what love was and felt empty and alone.

George had a series of relationships all through college, all
so dysfunctional that he began to isolate more and more,
feeling that relationships were a waste of time and painful. He
felt safer having sex with himself and his pornography collec-

tion. George realized that all his women were either alcoholic or food addicted and he couldn't understand why this was happening to him over and over again.

Eventually George met an attractive woman named Pam at an office party. She seemed nice enough so he thought he would risk asking her out. She loved to talk and he would just sit and listen to her. Something about her was very exciting and though he could not put his finger on it, he became more and more enchanted with her. Pam was very unpredictable and always seemed to be in the middle of one crisis or another. There was never a dull moment for George when he was with Pam. Like the other women he had dated, Pam was obsessed with her weight and her looks. She was always asking him if he thought she was pretty. He always said yes and wondered why she was so insecure about her physical appearances.

Pam and George decided to get married and both were looking forward to a happy life together. Pam did not have a father because her natural father had died when she was very young. She had been living with her older brother and mother before moving in with George. There was a great deal of tension between Pam and her brother and George asked Pam about it. Pam said that her brother had been very mean to her when they were growing up and had once forced himself on her when they were younger. She assured George that she is over it and that the sexual abuse never really affected her much.

The Marriage

After Pam and George moved in together, George noticed that Pam likes to have a couple of glasses of wine before she goes to bed to help her get to sleep. Sometimes she has more than a couple of glasses and gets very drunk. When she is drunk, she yells at George and tells him he is just like all other men. The morning after bouts such as this, she apologizes and prepares special meals and later has sex with him. Pam is in the beginning stages of alcoholism and has many unresolved family of origin issues. She had no fathering because of her father's early death and she was sexually abused by her brother.

Enter Sally

One day at the office George meets Sally, a new employee. He and Sally will be working closely together on a project. She is not only attractive but very interesting to talk to. Their project involves a lot of office time and he and Sally often work together late at night. When they do, they usually take a break for dinner. George becomes more and more attracted to her and fantasizes about her when masturbating or when he has sex with Pam. Eventually, he and Sally begin a sexual relationship and George now believes he has made a mistake by marrying Pam. Sally is very impressed with George's position in the office and is attracted to him physically. She is concerned about having an affair with a married man again because the last one was so painful.

Sally comes from a family in which both parents were extremely religious. Her father was a preacher and church had always been the center of the family's life. Sally has heard from her mother that her father was pretty wild in his youth and quite the ladies' man. She also heard from an aunt that her mother was very popular in school and had lots of dates. Sally always suspected that her parents had to get married, that her mother was pregnant with her sister, Lynn, but her parents deny it. Sally's mother was only 17 when Lynn was born and Sally had often thought that was strange. Lynn hated church as a child and later resented not being able to wear makeup or date boys as her friends did. Her father didn't let her date officially until she was 17 but she secretly had boyfriends much before then. She couldn't see why her mother was able to date before age 17 and she wasn't. Her father reminded her that she would not want to get a reputation for being loose.

Lynn had got pregnant at the age of 17 and had an abortion without her parents ever knowing about it. Sally and her sister had also acted out sexually together as children but her parents never knew about that either. Both Sally and her sister were sexually active from a very young age but careful about not letting their parents find out. Sally's parents were overprotective and at times Sally felt smothered. Her mother was always worried about her and would panic if either she or her sister became ill. One parent or the other would then give them enemas. This continued into adolescence and Sally always felt humiliated afterward.

Excessive use of enemas is sexually abusive and intrusive. Usually parents give them for health reasons but to a child it is a shameful experience. This type of abuse comes from the parents' lack of awareness and information. Most likely this procedure was performed within the parents' family of origin. Also, physicians frequently recommended enemas as recently as 20 years ago. During the 1940s, '50s and '60s, enemas were a very common prescription for childhood illnesses.

When Sally and her sister were younger, they shared a bedroom. Periodically, they would hear their parents fighting in the next room and sometimes their mother would come to their room to sleep in one of their beds. The mother would cry and hug Sally and Lynn and Sally remembers feeling awful at these times. Sally also remembers her mother hugging, crying and kissing her in bed and sometimes Sally felt uncomfortable with the way her mother touched her.

When touching feels wrong or uncomfortable, it is most likely inappropriate touching. If touching is painful, it is abusive. In this scenario, Sally's best interests are not considered. The mother has set up her daughters to take care of her emotionally. Her daughters, during these times, were not allowed to be children. They had to assume the role of mother's caretakers. Also the mother's physical touch during these times was sexually abusive. It is difficult to trust parents who are incapable of caring for themselves in a healthy way. Children cannot depend on them for care as long as the parents are emotionally childlike. Parenting a parent — in childhood — is a survival skill. There is a fear that the parent will not be there to give care and the children then work at "fixing" the parent. When children are nurturing or taking care of distressed parents and the parents abuse them sexually under the guise of needing love and nurturing, then the children will often make excuses for the abusive behavior. "Mother was feeling upset and just needed love. That's why she was hugging me like that." The rationalization, for the child, justifies the adult's behavior.

Sally suspected that the reason her parents fought was because her father had affairs with other women. This angered Sally, especially because he also spent a great deal of time in church activities. Sally felt that it was hypocritical for him to have love affairs while also preaching in church.

When an individual has a sexual relationship outside of their marriage, this is sexually addictive behavior. Whenever an adult sexually abuses a child with touch, be it painful or pleasurable to the child, this is also sexually addicted behavior on the part of the adult. In cases where the abusive touch has been pleasurable to the child, the sex addict may then justify the inappropriate sexual touch.

The child is confused. Resolution of abuse issues is difficult because the survivor finds it difficult to understand that the touch or sexual encounter *was* abusive since it felt pleasurable. *I liked it, so it wasn't wrong. — I liked it, so how can I be angry with the person who touched me?* These are obstacles in the way of the healing process because the victim doesn't feel justified in calling the experience abusive.

Sexual abuse that is pleasurable also sets up sex addiction. The abusive survivor sees the abusive experience as pleasurable and the pleasurable abuse experiences can cause our adult relationships to be dysfunctional. Sexual stimulation or sexual acting out becomes confused with love and intimacy. This inhibits the development of significant, healthy, long-lasting, intimate relationships. For some sex addicts abused this way in childhood, the potential is there for sexual abuse of their children or other minors. Since they see their own experience in a positive light, they will not see the behavior as abusive when inflicting it on others. Defenses such as denial, delusional thinking and rationalization may convince the addict that his or her behavior is loving and nurturing, when in fact it is abusive.

As noted earlier, there are many different types of sexually addictive behaviors and not all involve direct, offensive behav-

ior toward others. My experience is that few people compre-
hend the disease of sexual addiction. The majority I have
worked with professionally on these issues initially thought
that sexually addictive behavior only involves abusive sexual
behavior toward others.

Within the last decade, a new self-help support group has
emerged to address not only issues of sexual addiction, but to
offer support to those sexually addicted individuals in search
of ways to change their dysfunctional behavior. This group is
called Sex Addicts Anonymous and its primary purpose is to
assist sex addicts who wish to recover from their addictive
sexual pursuits. Sex Addicts Anonymous is modeled after
Alcoholics Anonymous and is based on the AA Traditions and
Steps for recovery from addiction. It is nonprofessional and it
is not therapy. The group's main purpose is to provide support
and information on the disease of sexual addiction. There is
a handout given to new members of Sex Addicts Anonymous
which describes the dynamics and characteristics of the disease of sexual addiction and its symptoms.

Characteristics Of Sexual Addicts

1. As adolescents, we used fantasy and compulsive masturbation to escape from feelings and we continued this
   behavior into our adult lives with compulsive sex.
2. We tended to become immobilized by romantic obses-
   sions.
3. We searched for some magical quality in others to make
   us feel complete. Other people were idealized and en-
   dowed with a powerful symbolism which often disappeared after we had sex with them.
4. Compulsive sex became a drug which we used to escape
   from feelings such as anxiety, loneliness, anger, rejection
   and self-hatred, as well as from joy. We sought oblivion
   in fantasy, masturbation and compulsive sex. Sex became
   a reward, punishment, distraction and time-killer.
5. Because of low self-esteem, we used sex to feel validated
   and complete.

6. We tended to lose ourselves in sex and romantic obsession and became addicted to the search for sex. As a result, we neglected our lives.

7. We tried to bring intensity and excitement into our lives with sex but instead found ourselves growing steadily emptier.

8. While constantly seeking intimacy with another person, the desperate quality of our needs made true intimacy impossible. In trying to conceal our dependency demands from ourselves and others, we grew more isolated and alienated from ourselves, from God and from the very people that we longed to be close to.

9. We feared relationships but continually searched for them. *In* a relationship, we feared abandonment and rejection but when *not* in one, we felt empty and incomplete.

10. We were drawn to people who were not available to us or who would reject and abuse us.

11. We often developed unhealthy dependency relationships that eventually became unbearable.

12. Even though we got the love of another person, it never seemed enough and we were unable to stop lusting after others.

13. We became addicted to people and were unable to distinguish between sex, love and affection.

S.A.F.E. — The Signs Of Compulsive Sexuality

1. It is a *Secret.* Anything that cannot pass public scrutiny will create the shame of a double life.

2. It is *Abusive.* Anything that is exploitative, harmful or degrading to self or to others will activate the addictive system.

3. It is used to avoid painful *Feelings.* If sexuality is used to alter moods or results in painful mood shifts, then it is clearly part of the addictive process.

4. It is *Empty.* There is no caring, committed relationship. Fundamental to the concept of recovery from addiction is the healthy dimension of human relationships. The addict runs a great risk by being sexual outside of a committed relationship.

Symptoms Of The Addiction Cycle

1. *Preoccupation:* The trance or mood wherein the addict's mind is completely engrossed with sex. This mental state creates an obsessive search for sexual stimulation.
2. *Ritualization:* The addict's own special routines which lead to the sexual behavior. The ritual intensifies the preoccupation, adding arousal and excitement.
3. *Compulsive sexual behavior:* The actual sex act, which is the goal of the preoccupation and ritualization. Sex addicts are unable to control or stop the behavior.
4. *Despair:* The feelings of utter hopelessness that addicts have about their behavior and their powerlessness.

This addiction, like all others, allows the addict to escape feelings of anger, pain, shame, loneliness and fear. It is also a dysfunctional shield and buffer from the realities of life. Sexual addiction affects both men and women and is not limited to any race or religion. It is present in all socioeconomic systems and does not care about education, profession or size of paycheck. It is very prevalent in our society though, the most hidden of the addictions. Looking back at the scenario of George and his relationship difficulties, we note that Sally's father, a preacher, is not excluded from this addiction in spite of his profession, his religious beliefs and his position in the community.

Religious Addiction

One consequence of sex-addicted family systems that is beginning to receive attention is the excessive use of religion. Religious addiction involves the use of religion as a means of escaping feelings, avoiding reality and justifying inappropriate behavior. Religious obsession is used at times in addictive family systems to hide the shame associated with abuse and addiction. In the eyes of the religious addict, excessive religious behavior will right the wrong. Unfortunately, religious addiction complicates matters of abuse and addiction even more. It delays the healing process from such dysfunction and sabotages any chance for true spirituality. It also causes confusion among those who have been abused: *"If they were such good church people, how could God let them abuse me?"* It is impossible to heal from abuse or addiction because the abuse or addiction is not acknowledged and individuals are shamed for having normal feelings of anger, grief and loneliness, all of which are necessary for healing.

When abuse or addiction is left unresolved, the experiences associated with these dysfunctions may eventually be forgotten or lost but the feelings about them are forever present. If these feelings are not processed, they are acted out in other behaviors which are dysfunctional and destructive and they are also passed on to the next generation. Religious addiction within sexually abusive and addictive family systems provides an unhealthy process of compensation for inappropriate sexual behavior. Religious addiction uses the tools of religion (i.e., the Bible, place of worship, God) as justification or rationalization for not fully experiencing healing and recovery by feeling all feelings. It *appears* to be an acceptable way to avoid taking responsibility for the pain and grief associated with abuse and addiction but in reality it is a wall built on shame. True spirituality requires feeling all feelings.

As we resolve and work through our unresolved family issues, we begin to discover what healthy spirituality is. By experiencing our rage, grief, loneliness and shame, we learn forgiveness of self and others. It is a challenging process but the rewards are overwhelming. Religious addiction is an ineffective shortcut which stunts spiritual growth. For individuals with abuse and addiction issues who come from religiously addicted families, the concept of spirituality has to be reexamined upon entry into recovery from family dysfunction.

I have worked with sexual abuse survivors who have admitted using religion as a means of surviving their suffering. They would acknowledge that they had been abused and quickly add that the abuse did not affect them any longer. They would also share with me that they had completely forgiven the abuser and were at peace with themselves. They would state that feelings of anger and sadness are negative and that they believed it important always to look at the positive side of life. Eventually I would have to tell them that the difficulties they were having in the here and now were directly related to their unfinished family of origin business and that their sexual abuse issues from childhood were still impacting their lives. I believe all our feelings are spiritual gifts that allow us to heal and learn from life. To deprive ourselves of any of our feelings is to *not* live life to its fullest. To hide from our past by means of addiction is to cheat ourselves out of experiencing all of the life process.

I have worked with several individuals who were sexually abused by members of the clergy whose denial of such abuse can be incredible. In one situation, I attempted to present to a clergy member who was guilty of such behavior some concepts of sexual addiction based on family of origin. This individual went into a rage. The church became his weapon. Many sexual addicts enter the clergy as a way of redeeming themselves of the shame associated with underlying sexual abuse issues and sexually addictive behavior. Unfortunately, their difficulties are not resolved, only disguised, destined to resurface eventually.

For those abused by clergy, the consequences are devastating. Clergy members are the teachers of spiritual principles and are perceived as the connection to God or a Higher Power. They are trusted servants and spiritual directors within their communities. They are in a position of authority in regard to spiritual matters. When this position of power is misused, the victims suffer not only sexual abuse but also spiritual abuse. The sex addict uses denial, rationalizations and delusional thinking to justify this behavior. I saw a phrase written on a church blackboard recently, "Family problems have roots and supports in the culture." I believe that is a most accurate statement. Our society perpetuates abuse from one generation to another by hiding behind addiction, delusion and denial. Abuse continues, not only directly but also indirectly due to society's denial. We have a responsibility to the next generation to address the many forms of child abuse that take place today in our homes, churches and schools. As long as abuse remains in the closet, addiction will continue in every social class, race, religious milieu and economic structure.

7

Recovery: What's A Couple To Do?

Law of Conservation
There are no secrets in a relationship. If a participant in a
relationship suppresses him or herself, then either they will
act out or the other participant will act out.

Sex Addicts Anonymous Newcomer's Handout

Secrets

Returning to the George and Pam scenario, it is easy to see
how addiction and family of origin issues can disrupt relationships. When we last spoke of George, he had started an
extramarital affair with Sally and was wondering if he had
made a mistake by marrying Pam. George does not know
how to have a healthy relationship, nor do Sally or Pam. All
three participants in this episode come from dysfunctional
family systems and suffer from a variety of addictions. They
are all continuing the dysfunctional traditions and behaviors
they learned in their families. If these issues are not dealt

with, they will pass the same traditions and behaviors on to the following generation, which may be disguised or acted out in slightly different activities but the dysfunction will still be there. Secrets that remain suppressed or hidden are always acted out by the members of the family system, specifically the children of that family system. If we do not address our own unfinished business, we will pass the feelings associated with that unfinished business on to our children. There is a saying, "A family is as sick as its secrets." I have seen this in action, both personally and professionally.

Periodically, parents bring their children to our office hoping that either Michael or I will have a quick solution to improper acting out, such as stealing, school phobias, eating disorders or any number of other difficulties. When the children are asked why they are stealing, for example, they usually reply, "I don't know." These children *really do not know* why they are behaving that way although they usually are aware something is wrong. When I ask how they are feeling, they appear confused, not understanding my question, because they are the product of families where it is not acceptable to feel all feelings. They are not allowed to have normal healing feelings of anger, pain and grief — *Go to your room until you can come out with a smile on your face — Don't be a cry baby — You should be grateful and stop pouting.* Feelings do not disappear when told to do so. They eventually emerge as dysfunctional behavior which may appear unrelated to buried feelings, unresolved issues, secrets. The parents of these children are totally focused on their child's acting out and cannot see the acting out as a response to their feelings about their past and their present dysfunction.

Most parents become uncomfortable when told this. When they begin looking at what their original family was like and how their current relationship with their spouse is going, the child's behavior is quickly understood.

If my son, Aaron, was having excessive temper tantrums, I would need to take a look at my relationship with Michael to see if some anger or other feelings in that relationship was not being addressed. If my relationship with Michael was clear of hidden anger issues, I would next need to see if I am avoiding any unfinished business from my past. Michael would also need to take a look at himself in a similar manner. If we both found we were not avoiding issues, it would certainly be appropriate to focus on Aaron. Usually, for us, when Aaron acts out excessively, there is some issue from the past or present in need of attention from Michael or from me — or from both of us in our relationship.

Children are not the only members in a family system who act out repressed dysfunction. If a spouse has a secret or is into an addiction and avoiding feelings, the other spouse will act out the feelings being avoided.

Referring back to George, while he is having an affair with Sally, Pam gains 15 pounds due to her compulsive eating or food addiction. Pam knows George is distancing himself from her but cannot understand why. She feels unattractive and wonders what she has done wrong. George is not honest with Pam about his feelings because he is avoiding his feelings with addictive behavior. He cannot resolve or honestly address his relationship with Pam. George is avoiding his difficulty in having a close honest intimacy with Pam and his fear of being vulnerable with her because his relationship with Sally is fun and exciting. Since there isn't a commitment involved, George knows he can leave the relationship whenever it becomes uncomfortable.

Pam thinks the problems are because of something she has done but she is not sure what that is because George does not talk honestly with her. Pam continues to overeat to avoid feeling the pain in her relationship with George. She does not talk honestly with George about it because she fears he will leave her. What she does do is to become more needy and demanding. When George is around Pam, he feels smothered. He knows Pam has a problem with food but it is never discussed. Pam's food addiction is a secret within the relationship and is just as powerful as George's secret about his affair. When Pam feels rejected and abandoned because of George's sexual acting out, she retreats into her addictive behavior with food. When George feels smothered, fearful and overwhelmed by Pam's neediness, he retreats to his sex-addicted behavior.

Each member of this relationship is equally responsible for the dysfunction within the system. The secrets, addictive behavior and unresolved family of origin business make it difficult for honest intimacy to develop. George and Pam can do one of two things in their present situation. Usually what couples do when confronted with issues such as this is for each one to focus on what the other is doing wrong or on what he or she is doing wrong to the other person. The focus becomes so extreme that they cannot find the perspective needed for looking within and healing.

George and Pam are accountable for their behavior and have a lot of healing work to do on their relationship before healthy trust and intimacy can be achieved. Before the relationship can be healed though, George and Pam will need to explore their original family issues to discover how they ended up in their present situation. Individual healing promotes healing within the relationship.

Sally, who participated in the extramarital affair with George, will need to explore her family to discover why she continually becomes involved in dysfunctional relationships. As long as she avoids her unfinished business, she will continue to have difficult relationships and will never know true intimacy. All three of these individuals, George, Pam and Sally, have unresolved abuse issues from childhood haunting them in their adult lives. The effects disrupt their chances for personal growth and sabotage any possibility for intimacy with another human being.

In order to recover, we need to ask ourselves some specific questions. We need to know the answers if we are to heal. It takes enormous courage but if we are persistent, we will reap the rewards of recovery.

Feelings: Then And Now

1. What do you do today when you get angry? _____

_____

2. What did you do as a child when you became angry?

_____

3. Did your parents allow you to be angry? ——————

4. What did they do or say to you when you became angry?
———————————————————————————

5. What does your wife/husband/significant other do or say when you become angry? ———————
———————————————————————————

6. Was it safe to be angry around your parents? ————

7. Is it acceptable or safe to be angry around your husband/wife/significant other? ———————————
———————————————————————————

8. What did your father do when he was angry?————
———————————————————————————

9. How did you feel about his anger? ——————
———————————————————————————

10. What did your mother do when she was angry? ———
———————————————————————————

11. How did you feel about her anger? ———————
———————————————————————————

12. What does your wife/husband/significant other do when angry? ————————————
———————————————————————————

13. How do you feel when they are angry? ——————
———————————————————————————

14. Do you see any similarities between your wife/husband/significant other and mother/father in relation to how anger is dealt with? ————————
———————————————————————————

15. Do you deal with anger the same way your mother or father did? _____
If so, like whom and how? _____

16. Were you ever physically abused (i.e., hit with a belt, slapped, etc.)? _____
How? _____
By whom? _____
How do you feel about it now? _____

Physical abuse is a destructive expression of anger. Many of us bear a lot of anger about being physically abused. If we do not face our feelings about this we may direct physical or emotional abuse at others. When a child is physically abused by an adult, that adult is behaving irresponsibly and is not handling his anger properly. Since the abusive adult is not owning his own anger, the abused child carries it into adulthood. This affects the way we process our anger here and now.

Some of us were shamed for being angry — *If you can't say something nice, don't say anything at all* — *If you're angry, just get busy and find something constructive to do.* Many of us were told we were bad for having angry feelings. Some of us were even punished for expressing our anger.

17. Think of an incident in your childhood when you were extremely angry. Write about that incident. _____
_____
_____
_____
_____

18. Did your parents know about it? _____ If they knew about it, how did they react to your anger? _____
_____

19. Think of a recent incident when you were extremely angry. Write about it. _____
_____
_____
_____

20. Did your wife/husband/significant other know about it? _____ If so, what was the reaction to your anger?

_____

_____

21. Are there any similarities in answers 18 and 20? _____

_____

22. Can you safely tell your parents today when you are angry? _____
How do they react? _____

23. Can you tell your parents when you are angry with them? _____
Do you protect them? _____

24. Do your parents talk to you about it today when they are angry with you? _____
How? _____

25. Do you know that it is normal and acceptable to be angry with those closest to us, from time to time? _____
Do you know that it is normal and acceptable to disagree with those closest to us at times? _____
Do you know that there is a difference between healthy and unhealthy fighting? _____

Rules For Fair Fighting

The following were developed for a family program at a treatment center called "The Meadows" in Wickenburg, Arizona, which specializes in co-dependency and relationship disorders.

- Be assertive rather than aggressive. Assertive is self-valuing. Focus on the *I* statements: *When you behave a certain way,* I *feel . . . Rather than: Your behavior sucks rotten eggs.*
- Have an appropriate sense of the other's dignity. No hitting below the belt.

- Stay in the *now* and avoid scorekeeping.
- Avoid judgment. Be aware of feelings.
- Be rigorously honest. Go for accuracy rather than agreement or perfection.
- Don't argue about extraneous details — *You're ten minutes late — No, I'm not, only seven.*
- Fight about one thing at a time.
- Repeat to the other person what you heard them say — you may not be sure or they may tell you that is not what they said.
- Don't assign blame. Rather, state your claim and exercise your power and responsibility of self.
- Unless you are being abused, hang in there.
- Be sure of who you really are angry with.
- Avoid questioning. You really can't argue with another person's reality or how they experience something.
- Be an active listener. Avoid interrupting.
- Speak freely, openly and directly.
- Don't threaten and don't panic about the noise level.
- Do realize that you have a right to your feelings, that they demand expression and that the same is true for others.

26. What do you do when you get sad or depressed now?
   _____

27. What did you do when you were sad, as a child? _____
   _____ Did you cry? _____

28. Did your parents allow you to be sad? Was it acceptable to be sad in your family from time to time? _____ Did your family allow you to cry? _____ Did you cry only when you were alone? _____

29. Did your parents know when you were sad? _____

30. How did your parents react to you when you cried? ____
   _____

31. Does your husband/wife/significant other consider it acceptable to be sad periodically? _____

32. Do you feel comfortable crying in front of your husband/ wife/significant other? _____
How do they react? _____

33. What did your father do when he was sad or depressed?
_____
Did you ever see him cry? _____ Did he feel comfortable letting you see him cry? _____ How did you feel seeing him cry? _____

34. What did your mother do when she was sad or depressed? _____
Did you ever see her cry? _____ Did she feel comfortable letting you see her cry? _____ How did you feel seeing her cry? _____

35. What does your wife/husband/significant other do when sad or depressed? _____
Ever cry in front of you? _____ Feel comfortable crying in front of you? _____ How do you feel when you see your wife/husband/significant other crying? _____

36. Do you see any similarities between your mother/father and your husband/wife/significant other in relation to how sadness is dealt with? _____

37. Do you deal with sadness the same way your mother/ father did? _____
If so, like whom and how? _____

38. Were you ever punished for crying or being sad? _____
If so, how? _____

39. Think of any incident during your childhood when you were very sad. Write about that incident. _____
_____
_____

40. Did your parents know about it? _____ If they knew about it, how did they react? _____
_____

41. Think of a recent incident when you were extremely sad or depressed. Write about it. _____
_____
_____

42. Did your wife/husband/significant other know about it? _____ If so, what was the reaction to your sadness?
_____
_____

43. Have you ever experienced the death of someone special to you? _____
If so, did you cry? _____ If you cried, did you cry in front of others or alone? _____

44. Have you ever been divorced? _____ If so, did you cry at any time during the divorce proceedings? _____

45. Do you know that it is natural to feel sad *anytime* we have a loss? _____ Do you know it is normal to grieve and feel sad when someone close to us dies, when we go through a divorce, when we change jobs, when we move to a different town, when our children leave home, when a pet dies, when we end a friendship, or when we experience any important change? _____ Do you know that crying allows us to heal from our loss and is necessary for our emotional growth and recovery? _____ Do you know that men need to cry just as much as women do? _____ If you have children, do you let them cry and have their sadness? _____

Grieving Our Pain

I believe we were provided with the ability to cry and grieve in order to heal from life's storms and hurts. Life is full of ups and downs and we need all our feelings to process the many experiences we have while on this great planet. Many of us grew up believing that the downs, the painful things in life, were to be buried and ignored. As a result, we never healed from the many losses of our childhood and early adulthood. Our pain can be a great teacher but if we have buried our sadness and grief, we can never benefit from their teachings. These buried traumas are affecting us today, disguised as addiction, loveless relationships, self-hate, intimacy problems, free-floating anxiety, depression, problems with regard to parenting and many other dysfunctions. When we do not heal from our past sadness, we carry it with us throughout our days.

Our unfinished business uses up the energy that would otherwise be available to experience the joys of life. If we do not allow ourselves our pain, we can never fully feel the joy of life but as we address our unfinished business, we open ourselves up to inner peace and serenity. If not faced, our unfinished business clutters our mind, leaving little room for the healthy, intimate relationship. It separates us from knowing ourselves and developing spiritually. Our unfinished business interferes with our ability to perceive the world as it really is and it creeps into our relationship with those closest to us. We end up replaying our unfinished business on those who are significant in our lives now. Women perceive all men as detached and unfeeling, or men perceive all women as excessively emotional and too needy. We keep on having the same dysfunctional connections over and over again with different partners — or we withdraw from forming relationships altogether, fearful of being hurt one more time.

Now that we know a little about how we learned about anger and grief, let's explore how we perceived our parents' relationship. At the same time we will look at our own relationships.

46. Did you ever see your parents fight or argue with one another? _____ Describe an incident you remember vividly. _____

    _____

    _____

    _____

47. Did either parent yell or rage at the other? _____ Did both parents rage while arguing? _____ If so, how did you feel then? _____

48. Was there ever any physical abuse between your parents while arguing? _____ Did you witness this? _____ Witnessing physical abuse is as damaging as being its target. If you witnessed physical abuse between your parents, did you ever have to break it up or protect one from the other? _____ If so, how did you feel at those times? _____ Having to protect one parent from another sets us up to be protectors or dysfunctional caretakers. As caretakers, we become involved with needy, over-dependent individuals who sometimes act helpless.

49. Did you ever witness either of your parents behaving destructively (i.e., throwing dishes, slamming doors, breaking furniture)? _____ If so, how did you feel during these times? _____ Witnessing a parent behave destructively is abusive. Children cannot feel safe when a parent is being destructive.

50. If your parents raged, but were not physically abusive, did you ever fear they would become destructive? _____ Whenever a parent rages, it is an inappropriate expression of anger and it is extremely damaging to those around them. When a parent rages, the dysfunctional behavior is called *rageaholism*. Rage-aholism intimidates those around the rager. The rager controls the family with raging behavior and other

family members will do whatever is necessary to keep the rager from acting out. It is frightening to be around a rageaholic and can deprive us of knowing how to express anger appropriately. We may find that we, too, rage, or we may stuff our anger, fearful of being like the rager we grew up with. Both are dysfunctional. We may also fear angry people and have difficulty in situations involving confrontation. Healthy anger allows us to protect and take care of ourselves. When we have healthy anger we feel motivated to stand up for ourselves in an assertive manner. If we rage, we feel shame afterwards, knowing at some level that our behavior was inappropriate. If we stuff our angry feelings, we walk around feeling helpless and victimized.

51. If your parents did not rage or yell, how did they express their anger toward one another? _____

_____

52. If they did not express their anger toward one another verbally, how did you know when they were in disagreement? _____

_____

Many of those I have worked with stated that their parents never argued. Our society looks upon this as an indicator of a healthy relationship when, in reality, it is an indicator of a dysfunctional relationship. Whenever a couple comes to our office and says, "We have never had a fight," I know immediately that the relationship is dysfunctional. Disagreement is a normal part of an intimate relationship. Not disagreeing is just as dysfunctional as raging. In a healthy relationship, the participants appreciate not only their own difference but the individuality of their partner as well. As human beings, we have many similarities but it is our differences that make us so interesting. We do not always have to like the differences but it is important to respect them.

Many people believe that they need always to stand together in agreement as a couple about everything. Individuality is lost and the fear of rejection and abandonment keeps both partners from expressing differing opinions. Though our society views this as healthy, it is in reality very dysfunctional. Those individuals are enmeshed with one another. This is also called *co-dependent behavior.* Resentment builds but is never resolved and the relationship lacks honest communication. Intimacy requires honesty. Censoring one's opinions creates distance and the participants never really know who the other is, creating a breeding ground for secrets that can destroy a relationship. Secrets are also acted out in the relationship, creating more confusion and distance between the partners. This is called *co-dependency.* How can you tell? The following is from the Co-dependents Anonymous *Newcomer's Handbook.*

- My good feelings about who I am stem from being liked by you.
- My good feelings about who I am stem from receiving approval from you. Your struggles affect my serenity. My attention is focused on solving your problems or relieving your pain.
- My attention is focused on pleasing you.
- My attention is focused on protecting you.
- My attention is focused on manipulating you to do things my way.
- My self-esteem is bolstered by solving your problems.
- My self-esteem is bolstered by relieving your pain. My own hobbies and interests are put aside. My time is spent sharing your interests and hobbies.
- Your clothing and personal appearance is dictated by my desires because I feel you are a reflection of me.
- Your behavior is dictated by my desires because I feel you are a reflection of me.
- I am not aware of how *I* feel. I am only aware of how *you* feel.
- I am not aware of what *I* want. I ask what *you* want.
- If I am not aware, I assume.
- The dreams I have for my future are linked to you.
- My fear of rejection determines what I say or do.

- My fear of your anger determines what I say or do.
- I use giving as a way of feeling safe in our relationship.
- My social circle diminishes as I involve myself with you.
- I put my values aside in order to connect with you.
- I value your opinion and your way of doing things more than my own.
- The quality of my life depends upon the quality of yours.

In a healthy relationship, each partner appreciates his own unique characteristics while at the same time respecting, though not always agreeing with the other's. People who never disagree fear doing so. It is safer to keep their opinions to themselves than to risk conflict. Usually individuals who never disagree haven't learned appropriate anger and see disagreement as wrong. When parents do not disagree verbally, children do not learn that confrontation is a normal part of the living experience. Also, when parents do not resolve the differences between them, their children will act out the unresolved feelings that the parents are ignoring. If mother is angry with father about an issue within the relationship and does not share it with father, the issue she has feelings about will not be resolved. Since the issue is not resolved, the feelings mother has about it will be buried.

As stated earlier, feelings do not disappear just because they are not faced. Unresolved feelings that are not addressed are acted out. Mother's angry feelings may be acted out by eating compulsively or one of the children may start fighting at school. Often the unresolved feelings within a relationship are acted out by the children of the family. They may start stealing, fighting, having sleep problems, eating compulsively or having other problems in school because of unexpressed feelings between their parents. Parents who rarely fight cannot understand why their children are having trouble. Usually, at such times, these parents will focus on the children's behavior, expecting the children to change, and not understanding that it is they who need to change. If our parents did not know how to disagree appropriately, we will not know how to have conflict or how to disagree appropriately in our adult life.

53. When you are angry with your husband/wife/significant other, what do you do? _____

54. Do you share with your partner when you are angry? _____

55. Do you feel very uncomfortable with or fear your partner's anger? _____ If so, why? _____

    Does your partner express anger the same way one of your parents did? _____ If so, which parent? _____ In what way is this similar?_____

56. Do you feel that you and your partner are able to resolve your disagreements?_____

57. List five issues that you and your partner disagree on regularly which have not been resolved.
    a. _____
    b. _____
    c. _____
    d. _____
    e. _____

58. Are any of the above issues similar to those that your parents have disagreed about? _____ If so, how? _____
    _____

When couples fight dysfunctionally, punishing one another is a tactic frequently used. Withholding sex, money, communication or physical touch are just a few of the ways dysfunctional couples punish one another.

59. In your relationships, how have you punished partners? _____
    _____

    How have you been punished by partners in relationships? _____

Did your parents ever punish one another? _____
If so, how? _____
Are there any similarities between the ways you and
your parents punished as a fighting tactic? _____

Many of us believe that for a disagreement to be resolved,
somebody has to win. As we grew up, for most of us, one of
our parents appeared to have more power than the other. But
just because somebody appears to win the battle doesn't
necessarily mean the issues have been resolved.

60. Who in your family had the most power? _____
How did you know this?_____
Who has the most power in your relationships, you or
your partner? _____
How do you know this? _____
Though winning an argument does not mean the issue
is resolved, who usually does win in your relationship?

How do you feel about this? _____
Do you feel the issues are resolved? _____
If not, do the issues eventually come up again? _____
Do you and your partner fight about the same issues
over and over again? _____

Many of the things that couples disagree about are disguised as new problems when in reality they are old issues
that have never been resolved. A healthy relationship is an
equal partnership; however, in many cases we end up fighting
with the same tactics that our parents used, hoping to win the
battle completely. Also, at times we find that we are disagreeing over the same issues that our parents never resolved. If
our parents were not able to resolve their differences, we
never had modeling for resolving differences in our relationships. This is why exploration into our family of origin is so
necessary. Our own history includes those conflicts that our
parents did not address and that, in many cases, they have

secrets about. Our parents' unfinished business has a direct effect on our adult relationships.

One area that most couples find troublesome is sex. In our society we are still not comfortable discussing sex. Most of us learn about sex and sexual relationships from our family of origin. Even if nobody in our family discussed it with us, we received a number of perceptions from our parents nonverbally. As children we observed our parents and saw how they interacted with one another and we developed our basic concepts about relationships. Sex is not just about the physical act itself. Sex involves the way we communicate with one another and how we see ourselves as sexual beings. Many of us experience the physical act of sex but do not feel connected with our partner, nor do we know how to appreciate ourselves as males or females.

I always knew I was female but for many years I was confused about what female is. I knew how to put makeup on and how to comb my hair but I didn't know how to appreciate my femaleness. If our same-sex parent was dysfunctional in any way, we did not receive all we needed to completely experience our own sexuality. If our mother did not know how to stand up for herself, we will not know how to be assertive. If father did not know how to be vulnerable and expressive, the male child will not know how to share pain. In order to start understanding ourselves as sexual beings, we must ask ourselves some very simple questions.

61. How did you learn about the physical workings of the sex act (at school, from parents, from friends)? _____

How old were you? ____ How did you feel about what you heard at that time? _____
Did you understand what was said? _____ Were you given any misinformation at that time? _____
If so, what? _____
If your parents did not give you complete information about sex, how do you feel about that now? _____

62. For Females: Who told you about menstruation? _____
Did you feel you were given enough information? _____
When you had your first menstrual cycle, were you
comforted and supported by your mother? _____
If not, how did you feel when you first menstruated?

_____

If you did not have enough information when you first
started menstruating, how did you feel? _____

_____

Write out your experience with your first menstrual
cycle._____

_____

_____

If you have a daughter, what about the above would
you change?_____

For Men Only: Who told you about female menstruation? _____ How did you feel about it? _____
Did it scare you? _____ At what age did you have your
first wet dream? _____ Did you understand what was
happening? _____ Did you have somebody with whom
to talk about it? Did you know this was part of adolescence or did you think you were doing something
wrong?_____

63. Did you masturbate as a child? _____ How did you
learn about this? _____ How often
do you remember masturbating? _____
How did you feel about masturbating? _____
_____ Did anyone ever punish or shame you
about masturbating? _____
Did you ever receive misinformation about masturbation — *You will go blind — become sterile — masturbation is dirty.*

As children develop, they discover that certain parts of
their bodies give them pleasure. Masturbation is a normal part

of child development. When masturbation becomes compulsive or excessive, it could be an indicator of childhood sexual abuse.

64. Did you ever act out sexually with other children, i.e., looking at another's genitals or showing your genitals to another? _____ Describe the incident or incidents.

_____

_____

Did you ever try to engage in physical sex with another child (excessive touching, intercourse, oral or anal sex)? _____ Did another child ever engage you in physical sex? _____ How do you remember feeling about this? _____ Did you ever tell anybody about this? _____

If older children engage younger children in sexual acting out, this may be sexually abusive depending on the ages and sexual experiences. Some sexual acting out during childhood is normal — *I'll show you mine if you show me yours* — but if the acting out progresses beyond that, there may be previous sexual abuse. If parents have sexual difficulties between the two of them and are not taking steps to deal with them, children may act out the sexual tension between the parents by excessive masturbation or excessive sex play with siblings or other children.

65. If your parents found out about your sexual acting out with others, describe what happened: _____

_____

_____

How did you feel? _____
Were you punished? _____ If so, how? _____

_____

66. Do you know if either of your parents had sexual relationships outside of their marriage? _____
Did you ever suspect that one of your parents was having an affair? _____ When a parent has an affair, this is sexual abuse toward the children in the family,

even if the children are not aware of the affair. It is abusive because the affair is a secret and, as a secret, it cannot be addressed and resolved. If an activity has to be kept secret, then the feelings associated with it will be acted out elsewhere in the family system.

67. Is it hard for you to see your parents as sexual beings? _____ Do you ever wonder if they enjoyed sex? _____ Did your parents regularly show affection towards one another by hugging, kind words or kissing in front of you? _____ If so, how? _____
Did either of your parents ever suggest that sex was dirty or bad — *Good girls don't* — *Bad boys do* — *You don't want to get a bad reputation* — *Sex before marriage is a sin* — *God will punish you.* _____ Did your parents ever use religion as a means of controlling your behavior? _____ *God will punish you for that* — *That is a sin.* _____ If so, how? _____

Did you ever fear that God would punish you for the way you behaved when you were growing up? _____ If so, how and for what? _____

Using God as a means of punishment is spiritually abusive. Children do a lot of magical thinking and when you tell a child that God is going to punish him for his behavior, he believes that God is going to hurt him. In later life, the belief will be, *God is going to get me — to hurt me.* In religiously addicted families, tactics such as these are common. Spiritual abuse stunts healthy emotional, sexual and spiritual development. Parents who repress their own sexuality may have come from spiritually abusive or religiously addicted homes. Also, parents who repress their sexuality may be sexual abuse survivors themselves from sex-addicted and/or alcoholic or drug-addicted families. Many survivors of emotional, physical and sexual abuse turn to excessive use of religion as a means of coping with their dysfunction This does not heal the experiences and feelings. It is a dysfunctional survival tactic which prevents healing and true spiritual development.

68. Do you remember a time in your childhood when someone touched you inappropriately on your genital or breast area? _____ If so, who touched you? _____ _____ Describe the incident. _____

_____

How do you feel about it now? _____
What age were you when this happened? _____ Have you ever told anyone about this? _____

If touching doesn't feel right or if it feels uncomfortable, it is probably abusive touching. When a child is sexually abused with inappropriate touching, sexual development may be halted. For many sex addicts, sexual fantasy may involve sexually abusive experiences from childhood which are disguised so as not to appear to be the consequence of abuse. For example, if a young male is sexually abused with fondling of the penis, consequences in adulthood may involve fantasies of being fondled. The excessive fantasy keeps the addict disconnected from sex partners and true intimacy cannot be established. The young girl who only experiences physical touch while being sexually abused may grow up believing the only way to experience physical touch is by being sexual. Sex and love become confused and the fantasy of being loved involves being sexual. True intimacy in this situation cannot be achieved.

69. Do you remember a time during childhood when someone performed oral or anal sex on you? _____ If so, describe the incident. _____

_____

How did you feel about it then? _____
How do you feel about it now? _____
Did anyone ever have sexual intercourse with you when you were a child? _____ If so, how did you feel about it then? _____
How do you feel about it now? _____

If we have been sexually abused as children, it is necessary that we heal from the experience so that we can enjoy healthy intimacy with others. Early incidents of sexual abuse have a direct impact on our adult lives. Many of us think these experiences no longer affect us today and this is called *denial*. If you are a sex abuse survivor, I strongly suggest that you attend Sexual Abuse Anonymous support groups or talk with a therapist who understands sexual abuse issues. The addresses for incest survivor support groups are Survivors of Incest Anonymous, P.O. Box 21817, Baltimore, Maryland 21222 and Sexual Abuse Anonymous, P. O. Box 80085, Minneapolis, Minnesota 55408.

Sexual Addicts Anonymous is another support group which is useful for addressing issues of sexual abuse as they relate to sexual addiction. The address for Sexual Addicts Anonymous is: Twin Cities S.A.A., P. O. Box 3038, Minneapolis, Minnesota 55403 (phone 612-339-0217).

There are also support groups for individuals who are co-dependent on sexual addicts (COSA). Co-dependent relationships in this situation are dysfunctional involvement with sex addicts. Co-dependents involved with sex addicts are usually sex abuse survivors and issues relating to sexual abuse and dysfunctional relationships are discussed in the groups. For more information, write to: Twin Cities COSA, P. O. Box 14537, Minneapolis, Minnesota 55408.

Another group that offers support to sex addicts and their co-dependents is called Sex and Love Addicts Anonymous (SLAA). Here, support is offered for relationship difficulties. Sexual abuse is also discussed. The address for SLAA is: The Augustine Fellowship, Sex and Love Addicts Anonymous, Fellowship-Wide Services, Inc., P. O. Box 119, New Town Branch, Boston, Massachusetts 02258.

70. Have you ever suspected that you were sexually abused? _____ After reading the information provided on sexual abuse in this book, do you think you may be a sexual abuse survivor? _____

With some understanding of how our unresolved family of origin problems have affected our lives, it is time to take a closer look at our present relationship. Earlier, I stated that one of the consequences of sexual abuse, in addition to sex addiction, is co-dependent behavior with sexual addicts. Co-dependent behavior with sex addicts is not only painful for the co-dependent but also enables the sex addict to continue acting out addictively. When a co-dependent enables sexually addictive behavior, chances of recovery of the sex addict and the co-dependent are limited.

According to the support group for co-dependency on sex addicts, some of the characteristics of an enabler of a sex addict are:

- Constantly thinks/obsesses about the sex addict's behavior and motives.
- Attempts to limit or control the addict's acting out, e.g., by handling all the social engagements and exerting influence to stop the acting out.
- Fears sexual involvement because of negative experiences in the past.
- Lies about, covers up or minimizes the sex addict's behavior.
- Has mounting anxiety about the addict's acting out.
- Feels inadequate about sex and sexual relationships.
- Exhibits insane or strange behavior and loses memory of it.
- Behavior is destructive to self and others.
- Has frequent accidents or other dangerous incidents which are caused by preoccupation with the sex addict and attempts to control him or her.
- Changes clothes out of the sight of spouse.
- Wears additional layers of clothing to divert sexual advances.
- Checks the sex addict's personal mail, journal, briefcase, etc.
- Wears clothes to satisfy the sex addict's wants.
- Shames the sex addict to control his or her behavior.
- Experiences free-floating shame and anxiety attacks.
- Accepts the label of *problem person.* Accepts responsibility for improvement of partner's sexual satisfaction.
- Uses sex as a reward for reconciling after fights, disagreements, etc.

- Focuses on the people or objects he acts out with rather than focusing on his own feelings about the acting out.
- Numbs own sexual needs and wants.
- Accepts partner's sexual norms as own norms.
- Changes geographical location to avoid the object of the addiction.
- Has a baby to recement the relationship.
- Makes excuses not to be sexual.
- Believes that sex is the only way to be intimate.
- Seeks sexual intimacy with partners before other kinds of intimacy are developed.
- Checks up on the sex addict's activities — plays detective.
- Feels distant/distracted/discontented/angry during sex.
- Is over-responsible and feels self-righteous about it.
- Keeps constantly busy as a distraction.
- Relies on material goods as the only indicators of a relationship.
- Accepts the label of crazy person and thinks, "I must be imagining things."

Newcomer Handout for Co-dependency on
Sexual Addicts Anonymous Support Groups (CoSA)

Co-dependents involved with sexual addicts are in need of just as much help as are the sex addicts themselves. In sexually addictive relationships, unresolved issues and resentments build up for both partners in the course of the relationship. Both are from family systems which were dysfunctional and, in most cases, sexually abusive. The abuse may have been subtle, resulting from lack of awareness and information, or it may have been intentional and obvious. Whatever the case, both partners in the sexually addictive relationship are responsible for exploring their own unresolved family of origin dysfunction. The dysfunction within the current relationship may be emotionally painful and even abusive but the key to understanding present relationships is in understanding the families of origin. As we work through our unfinished business with our original families, we will make healthy decisions about our current relationships.

The degree of difficulty in our current relationships is indicative of the amount of dysfunction in our own family of origin. Let's take a look at our adult sexual history.

71. Describe your first sexual experience. _____
_____
_____

How old were you? _____ Did you enjoy it? _____
Did you have to drink alcohol or use mood-altering chemicals before your first sexual encounter? _____
Was your first sexual encounter what you thought it would be? _____ If you could do it over again, what would you change about your first sexual encounter?
_____
_____

72. How many sex partners have you had up to this point? _____ What is it about the act of sex that you enjoy?
_____
_____

Is there anything about the act of sex that you dislike?
_____
_____

What sexual behaviors do you find the most pleasurable? _____
_____

Does your partner enjoy these behaviors? _____
If not, how do you feel about that? _____
Can you and your partner discuss likes and dislikes about sex openly? _____
What information about your sexual relationship do you fear sharing with your partner? _____
Do you ever feel used by your partner while having sex (as though all your partner wants is your body for sexual acting out)? _____ Do you ever feel that you use your partner's body for the sake of physical sex? _____ Do you engage in sexual activity with a partner you feel uncomfortable with? _____ If so,

describe the behavior. _____
_____

73. Do you or your partner ever use pornography or X-
    rated videos to stimulate or promote your sexual en-
    counter? ____ How do you feel about this? _____
    Do you or your partner have pornography available to
    be used to stimulate sexual excitement while mastur-
    bating alone? ____ Do you fantasize about others on a
    regular basis while having sex with your partner? ____
    If so, what do your fantasies consist of? _____
    _____
    Do you feel comfortable sharing these fantasies with
    your partner? ____ If not, why? _____
    _____
    Do you require that you or your partner dress in a
    particular way or act a certain way in order for you or
    your partner to be more sexually attractive? ____ If so,
    describe how. _____
    _____

74. Does your partner ever complain about your sexual de-
    mands or comment about your sexual appetite? _____
    If so, is the complaint about too much sexual appetite
    or too little? _____ If complaints involve too much de-
    mand for physical sex, do you ever accuse your partner
    of being old-fashioned or not *with it* sexually, instead
    of considering the possibility that you or your partner
    may be sexually addicted? _____ Does the above state-
    ment make you feel angry or ashamed? _____
    If so, you may be a sexual addict. If your partner
    complains about your lack of sexual appetite, you may
    be married to a sex addict or you may be a sexual
    abuse survivor or a sex addict yourself. Many sex ad-
    dicts find sex with self through masturbation safer
    emotionally than risking vulnerability during sex with a
    partner. If masturbation replaces intimate sexual contact
    with a relationship partner, the masturbation is an indi-
    cator of sexual addiction. Do you ever feel that if you

and your partner had better sex, your relationship over-
all would be improved? _____

75. Do you feel disconnected emotionally from your sex
partner during sex? _____ How do you feel about this?
_____
Do you fear telling your partner about this? _____
Are you afraid to share your concerns about your sexual
relationship with your partner, for fear of being rejected
or abandoned? _____ If you haven't shared your concerns with your partner, what concerns would you like
to share with your partner? _____
_____
_____
Have you ever shared with anyone else your concerns
about your relationship with your partner? _____
Do you avoid, cover up or minimize dysfunction in
your current relationship to yourself and to others?
_____

76. Have you ever had a physical, sexual affair outside of a
significant relationship? _____ If so, did you ever tell
anyone about it? _____ How do you feel about it now?
_____
Have you ever been involved with a partner who had a
physical, sexual affair outside of a relationship with
you? _____ If so, how did you feel about it? _____
_____
Do you feel the issue was completely resolved or do
you still have feelings about it? _____ Did you confront your partner or keep quiet about it? _____ If you
kept quiet about the affair, you enabled your partner's
sexually addictive behavior.

77. Do you feel more comfortable sharing your problems
and concerns with members of the opposite sex? _____
Do you share things with members of the opposite sex
that you do not share with your relationship partner?
_____ Have you had close relationships with members

of the opposite sex, outside of your main relationship, which felt safer than your significant relationship? _____ If so, how did they feel safer? _____

_____

_____

Whenever we are getting our intimacy needs taken care of outside of our marital or significant relationship, we are involved in an affair. A sexual affair involves getting both our emotional and sexual needs taken care of outside of our primary relationship. An emotional affair involves getting only our emotional need for intimacy taken care of outside our primary relationship. As long as we are filling our sexual and emotional intimacy needs elsewhere, we do not have to address why we do not or cannot do so within the primary relationship.

Work For Recovery: Separately And Together

A healthy relationship requires a great deal of work. Some people in a dysfunctional relationship will abandon the relationship, believing that by distancing themselves from their partner they will also escape the suffering. They believe the partner was totally responsible for the distress in the relationship and that when the partner is no longer around, the pain will be alleviated. Eventually, another partner fills the shoes of the previous mate and all appears well for a while, but the problems of the previous relationship will reappear and there is confusion about how this could happen again. They may move from one relationship to another, not seeing that their family of origin history is responsible for their misery.

Others cope with the dysfunction by settling for the way things are, unaware that a wonderful world of intimacy and self-discovery awaits, if only they would look for it. They keep busy, find distractions to avoid confronting the lack of intimacy. They feel trapped, not knowing there is a way out of their loveless situation which does not necessarily require abandoning their partner.

Recovery is available for both partners but in order to recover, both partners must first start to heal individually. Both must focus away from each other and focus on their own unfinished family business. A relationship is a partnership and no partner is completely responsible for all the grief in it. In order to grow, we must each first clear away the wreckage of the past. It is not an easy thing to do but the recovery process brings more gifts than can be imagined. As we recover, we will develop a better understanding of our present and past relationships.

In recovery we learn to take care of ourselves, not expecting others to do it for us. We learn how to share who we are by being vulnerable and imperfect. In recovery we learn to respect others and, most importantly, ourselves — by not accepting abusive behavior from anyone. Recovery involves learning that we do not always have to agree with our partner and our partner does not always have to agree with us. What makes us each so unique as human beings is that we all see things differently and this is part of what makes our relationships precious. Disagreement forces us to keep an open mind, to define who we are as individuals and continue to grow. With recovery, we also learn that physical sex does not make intimacy but enhances it. Healthy physical sex is just a part of an intimate relationship for which both partners are responsible.

Recovering as a couple takes much courage. The grief and resentments of the relationship take time to resolve and trust is not built overnight. Patience is the key to a successful recovery for a couple. It is a hard process. Angry feelings surface as both partners start to share their feelings about the relationship. Commitment is needed. Threats — *I'll leave.* — *Let's get a divorce.* — when the pain of the process hits, it can sabotage any healthy resolution of the resentments and unconfronted feelings. If a couple is to recover together, they must commit to the relationship for a period of time which they specify and agree to. During this period they commit to no mention of abandoning the relationship for six months to a year. After that, they may re-evaluate and decide to either continue the relationship or end it.

Even if the decision is to end the relationship, at least both partners will have had time, hopefully, to explore their family of origin dysfunction which set up the difficulties.

If one member refuses to explore, at least the other will have some understanding of why the relationship did not work and so be better prepared for the next. Having seen how family of origin issues set up the dysfunction within the ended relationship and after a period of grieving over its loss, the chances are good for a successful, healthy, intimate experience in the future.

Learning how to be intimate teaches us about ourselves. Relationships do not make us complete or fill our emptiness. It is our job to learn how to be whole human beings, capable of parenting ourselves. As we learn how to nurture and love ourselves, we will also learn how to nurture and love others. Love is an overused word, much misused in our society because few people know what it means. Love begins by learning how to appreciate and accept who *we* are, with all of our own talents and imperfections. Growth is a part of the human experience and as we continue to develop emotionally and spiritually, we learn to appreciate the experience of living. I believe there is hope for many relationships in trouble. I wish that you, the reader, will have the courage to begin your own personal journey on the road to recovery, whether or not your partner chooses to follow.

8

Toward Healthy Intimacy[*]

Since we act out our unfinished family of origin business with those closest to us, it is important to examine those characteristics that our mates have in common with our parents. By exploring this dynamic, we can see how our unfinished business affects and interferes with our ability to be intimate in healthy ways. It is important to look at the personal characteristics of both past and present partners. To see how we continue to pick partners similar to our parents, we begin by listing our parents' characteristics along with those of our current and past partners.

Table 8.1. Which Parent Are Your Partners Most Like Characteristically?
Example one: Comparing parental characteristics with partners' characteristics

Traits	Father	Mother	First Wife	Second Wife
Physical traits	Tall, dark complect, attractive, overweight, dark hair	Tall, dark complect, attractive, underweight, long dark hair	Tall, dark complect, attractive, underweight, dark short hair	Tall, light complect, attractive, underweight, long dark hair
Emotional traits	Difficulty expressing feelings, loner, detached, withdrawn, silent	Emotional, needy, critical, demanding, hyper-sensitive, very social	Emotional, needy, strong need for approval, depressed	Emotional, needy, very insecure, demanding, critical
Known, suspected or possible addictions	Workaholic, sex addict, eating disorder, co-dependent	Chemically dependent, eating disorder, co-dependent	Chemically dependent, eating disorder, co-dependent	Chemically dependent, eating disorder, co-dependent
Family of origin history	Father died early in life from cancer, mother was alcoholic	Father was alcoholic and sexually abusive, mother was an incest survivor	Father was sexual addict, mother had an eating addiction	Father was sexually abusive and alcoholic, mother was alcoholic

Table 8.2. Which Parent Are Your Partners Most Like Characteristically?
Example two: Comparing parental characteristics with partners' characteristics

Traits	Mother	Father	First Boyfriend	Second Boyfriend
Physical traits	Tall, dark hair, dark complect, overweight	Short, blond hair, light complect, weight approp.	Short, blond hair, light complect, overweight	Short, blond hair, light complect, weight approp.
Emotional traits	Rager, angry, manipulative, rigid	Rager, angry, controlling, abusive	Loud, angry, controlling, abusive	Rager, angry, controlling, abusive
Known, suspected or possible addictions	Workaholism, religious addict, rageaholic	Rageaholism, alcoholic, sex addict	Workaholism, rageaholic, sex addict	Alcoholism, rageaholic, sex addict
Family of origin history	Father was religious addict, dry alcoholic, mother was a religious addict	Father was abusive and alcoholic, mother was an incest survivor and rageaholic	Father was an alcoholic and sex addict, mother was a workaholic and rageaholic	Father was a workaholic and sex addict, mother was a religious addict with an eating disorder

Table 8.3. Fill In The Boxes With The Characteristics Of Your Partners And Parents

Traits	Father	Mother	First Partner	Second Partner
Physical traits				
Emotional traits				
Known, suspected or possible addictions				
Family of origin history				

What similarities do you see?

1. _____   4. _____   7. _____
2. _____   5. _____   8. _____
3. _____   6. _____   9. _____

Table 8.4. Which Parent Are You The Most Like? Example one: For a female

Traits	Father	Mother	Self
Physical traits	Tall, overweight, light complect, dark hair	Short, underweight, light complect, light hair	Tall, overweight, light complect, light hair
Emotional traits	Social, detached, difficulty feeling feelings, critical	Withdrawn, overreactive, depressed, needy, insecure	Withdrawn, overreactive, depressed, needy, insecure
Known, suspected or possible addictions	Eatng disorder, sex addict, co-dependent	Eating disorder, work addict, co-dependent	Eating disorder, drug addicted, co-dependent
Family of origin history	Father was sex addict, mother had eating disorder	Father was alcoholic, mother was addicted to Valium	

Table 8.5. Which Parent Are You The Most Like? Example two: For a male

Traits	Mother	Father	Self	
Physical traits	Short, blond hair, light complect, underweight	Average height, dark complect, dair hair, average weight	Average height, dark complect, dark hair, underweight	
Emotional traits	Angry, abusive, self-centered, low self-esteem	Timid, hesitant, depressed, loner	Timid, shy, guarded, angry	
Known, suspected or possible addictions	Prescription drug addiction, anorexic, rageholic	Workaholic, co-dependent, sex addict	Alcoholic, co-dependent, sex addict	
Family of origin history	Father was very co-dependent and sexually addicted, mother was a compulsive eater	Father was an alcoholic and workaholic, mother was a sex addict who left father for another man		

Table 8.6. Fill In The Boxes With The Characteristics Of Yourself And Your Parents

Traits	Mother	Father	Self	What similarities did you discover?
Physical traits				1. _____ 2. _____
Emotional traits				3. _____ 4. _____ 5. _____
Known, suspected or possible addictions				6. _____ 7. _____
Family of origin history				8. _____

After we have seen what characteristics our parents and our partners have in common, it is important to discover if we are punishing our mates for our unresolved feelings toward our parents. Unresolved issues with parents may include:

1. Abandonment: lack of attention, physical or emotional unavailability.
2. Verbal abuse: name calling — stupid, dumb, incompetent, lazy, selfish, unworthy, etc.
3. Demanding perfection in appearance, behavior, not allowing natural mistakes, being excessively critical.
4. Overcontrolling social activities, dress, friendships.
5. Not allowing expression of feelings of anger, grief, pain, or even joy.
6. Not setting limits, not being consistent, not being clear about wants.
7. Physical abuse: slapping, shaking, whipping with belt or other objects, pushing, hair pulling.
8. Shaming: degrading punishments.
9. Sexual abuse: forcing sexual behavior, sexual name calling — whore, slut — engaging in extramarital affairs.
10. Spiritual abuse: using God, the Church, the Bible as basis for threats; calling behavior sinful; comments such as, "God would want you to do this."

Unresolved issues with our parents will continue to affect our current relationships until we address them and *have* our feelings about them. Also we may find that we either punish or control our mates the way our parents punished or controlled us or we may be involved with someone who punishes or controls us similarly.

If we are survivors of sexual, physical or emotional abuse, we will have difficulty taking care of ourselves in a healthy manner in our relationships. We don't know how to set appropriate limits within relationships and we tend to operate in extremes.

In my relationship with Michael, I would overfeel and believed I was responsible for all painful situations experienced by those closest to me. If they were upset for any reason, I would immediately feel responsible for their pain, as though I was in some way at fault or the cause of the upset.

Michael, at the other extreme, had difficulty feeling any feelings and rarely expressed sadness or anger. To watch the two of us before we began our individual healing was curious — comical at times. We visit friends and relatives regularly and several years back when we were just about to open our private practice together, comments were made about Michael's questionable ability to manage a business. This happened a number of times and each time Michael would just laugh it off. Sometimes the comments were very shaming and I would be in a rage about them for several days. Now, mind you, these comments were not directed at me but I was the one who was angry about them, while Michael went on as if nothing had been said. What was actually happening was that Michael did not know how to feel feelings and since I felt overly responsible for the pain of others, I would take up the fight and feel his feelings for him. While ranting, raving and suffering about what had been said to Michael, I was enabling Michael to not experience his own anger about the shaming comments. Michael would say to me, "Why should I get upset about these comments when you're more than angry enough for the two of us?"

By fighting Michael's cause and feeling his feelings I did not have to address how my own abilities as a business woman had been discounted. By not focusing on how my skills had been ignored, I missed an opportunity to heal my own unresolved hurt about being intellectually discounted when I was a child. Aside from avoiding my unfinished business, I was enabling Michael to not be responsible for his feelings of anger at being shamed and I was also enabling him to not explore his unfinished business.

When I raged or became hopelessly depressed from feeling not only my own feelings but also Michael's, his attention would always be directed to my over-reactive behavior. He would accuse me of being too emotional and of going over-board with my feelings; I would accuse him of being an insensitive cold fish who didn't react at all. Then the big fight would begin and we would both be so focused on each other that at times we didn't know what had started the conflict. Because we constantly focused on each other's behavior and our own feelings about that behavior, we rarely, if ever, resolved a disagreement. Unresolved resentments put distance between the partners in a relationship and, as a result, trust and intimacy cannot flourish.

When we were angry with one another I fought with him the way my mother did with my father. He would fight the way his father did with his mother. Eventually, we would fight about the way we were fighting and nothing was resolved. It was important for each of us individually to explore our parents' relationships to see how we were acting out their relationships with each other. Many things about our parents' relationships were dysfunctional and we were continuing the dysfunction in ours. We had to examine these relationships so as to begin changing ours.

Eventually, long after a great deal of family of origin exploration, I discovered why I felt others' feelings and Michael learned why he had difficulty feeling feelings.

I had to learn how to set limits and not be responsible for anybody's feelings except my own while Michael had to learn how to be responsible for his own feelings, not letting others feel them for him. As a result, we are both able to be more attentive to our own unfinished business and present problems. By concentrating on ourselves, we are more often able to resolve our disagreements in a healthy manner. Instead of fighting our parents' fights, we can target our own feelings about the difficulties in our relationship. When resolution to disagreement is reached, the successful process of resolution breeds true intimacy and mutual respect.

I am responsible for setting limits with others in a healthy manner and taking care of myself, regardless of the situation. For those of us who have been abused, this seems unrealistic and impossible. We either feel continually victimized or we offend and abuse others. Many of us know how to survive as victims. When we are abused we may disassociate or numb out emotionally or seek the help of food, work, alcohol, drugs, religion, sex, compulsive spending or any number of other dysfunctional behaviors. Some of us continue as adults to be emotionally, physically — even sexually — abused by our partners. We tell ourselves that it really isn't that bad and we minimize the dysfunction. Growing up, we learned to survive with abuse but these same survival tools which kept us sane then are keeping us from enjoying healthy, intimate relationships now.

What inappropriate, abusive or dysfunctional behaviors are you encountering from your partner now that make you feel bad emotionally, physically or sexually? List five.

a. _____
b. _____
c. _____
d. _____
e. _____

What would happen if you said *no* or told your partner that you are no longer willing to accept these behaviors? _____
_____
_____
_____

One consequence of taking care of ourselves in our relationships is increased confrontation and confrontation clears up unresolved resentments and makes way for healthy intimacy. We must be responsible for setting limits and not accepting unacceptable behavior, even sexually. One of the most difficult words we have to learn in recovery is *no.* If we continue to participate in activities with our partners which we feel are unacceptable or which make us uncomfortable, we will eventually be full of resentment not only toward our partner but also toward ourselves.

What behaviors or comments by your partner cause you pain? List four.

a. _____
b. _____
c. _____
d. _____

What can you do to take care of yourself with regards to these issues? _____

_____

I am a recovering rageaholic. For years, I expressed anger by yelling at the top of my lungs. One day Michael decided that he was enabling my behavior by accepting my raging and not taking care of himself. We were in a restaurant and I was just building to a rage when he got up and left me there. By taking care of himself, Michael was not enabling me to act out with raging. I was forced to accept that my raging behavior was inappropriate and to take responsibility for seeking help for this dysfunction.

When we allow someone to abuse us emotionally, we are not making them accountable for their dysfunctional behavior. Harsh criticism or shaming remarks can be as painful as physical abuse and to accept them is to avoid being responsible for our own well-being. Individuals who are emotionally offensive, shaming or hypercritical have a family of origin where they, too, were emotionally abused. They become adults who are emotionally abusive to their spouses and their children.

Do you see yourself as emotionally abusive, shaming or hypercritical? _____ If so, please list incidents of abuse:

   a. _____
   b. _____
   c. _____
   d. _____

Do you see your actions as the result of your unresolved childhood emotional abuse? _____ If so, who abused you and how? _____

_____

Do you ever use silence as a way of getting back at your partner? _____ If so, this is emotionally punitive. Did either of your parents use silence or withhold affection from you as a punishment? _____ If so, who? _____
Describe an incident. _____

_____

To use silence as a way of punishing or getting back at a partner is hurtful in that it is discounting and shaming. It also sets a partner up to avoid communicating honestly, for fear of being rejected and abandoned. It is as detrimental as raging and it prevents healthy resolution of disagreements, which precludes intimacy.

Our physical bodies and the care of our bodies are our responsibility. It is our job to keep ourselves safe. If we were abused as children, our tools for protecting ourselves physically may be limited, but even if we have a limited ability to keep ourselves physically safe, it is still our responsibility to learn how. Has a partner, past or present, ever done anything to your body that made you feel physically uncomfortable (pushing, hitting, slapping, shoving, pinching)? If so, please list these incidents.

a. _____
b. _____
c. _____
d. _____

Is there *anything* you could have done to prevent or stop those offenses (called police, left, gone to a friend)?

a. _____
b. _____
c. _____
d. _____

Individuals who are mistreated in a relationship usually were mistreated as children as well. They never learned how to stand up for themselves and take care of themselves. Since they had no choice then, they don't see a choice now. Allowing someone to be physically hurtful is to enable dysfunctional behavior.

Individuals who are physically destructive have also been mistreated as children and they are doing to others now what was done to them. Have you ever been physically abusive to a past or present partner or to your children? _____ If so, list incidents.

a. _____

b. _____

c. _____

d. _____

If you are in the habit of physically attacking your partner or your children, I strongly suggest that you seek psychological help. Abusive behavior is a serious consequence of unresolved childhood abuse issues and the result can be devastating, not only to others, but to self.

Do you see your pattern of being physically abusive as the result of your own unresolved childhood abuse? _____ If so, who physically abused you and how? _____

_____

_____

For those of us who were sexually harmed or for whom issues surrounding sex were never made clear, adult sex can be confusing — sometimes even emotionally painful. We may confuse sex with love. For those of us who are sexually addicted, the act of sex is based on fantasy and our ability to connect emotionally with our sexual partner is limited. Our sexual development has gotten stuck.

For those living with a sexual addict, feelings of confusion and resentment which are rarely spoken of, not only distance us emotionally from our partners, but also separate us from ourselves. We may be confronted with demands for too much physical sex or we may wonder why our partner chooses to not have sex with us more often. We dress up, act out and perform sexually with our partner in behaviors that may not appeal to us and in some cases are repulsive to us. But most of us do not share these feelings with our partner for fear of rejection or abandonment. So we continue to enable sexually addictive behaviors and we cover up our own pain in addictive behavior with food, work, drugs, alcohol and more.

Addiction in any form can destroy a relationship. Most of the time both partners focus on the other aspects of the relationship such as job, money, children, in-laws — avoiding discussion of the addiction altogether. The belief is that if

Table 8.7. Example Of The Progression Of Addiction For Both Partners In A Dysfunctional Relationship

Eating Disorders	Sexual Addiction
Diuretics, laxatives, fasting, vomiting	Pornography, videos, fantasy, magazines, movies used to stimulate sexual acting out
Food blackout	Masturbation begins to replace sexual relationship with mate
Continuous eating	Emotional or physical affairs outside of main relationship
Hiding food	Sexual fantasy used more often as a method of escape
Eating alone, eating in car	Difficulty being vulnerable during sex
Weight fluctuations	Feeling distant during sex from sex partner
Continuous dieting	Sex with mate becomes mechanical and void of feeling
Compulsive exercising	Over-use of fantasy during sex, having sex with a fantasy instead of with partner
Calorie counting	Using sex to make up after fighting or to replace intimacy
Fear of being fat	
Obsession with body and appearance	
Feeling insecure and unattractive	
Difficulty trusting	

Characteristics of a Dysfunctional Relationship

Lack of appropriate boundaries   Lack of intimacy
Co-dependent caretaking behavior   Lack of communication
Fear of abandonment   Lack of tolerance for individual differences

Progression Of Addiction

Table 8.8. Psychosexual Development

CHILDHOOD SEXUALITY/Experimental Stage	ADOLESCENT SEXUALITY/Seeking Stage	ADULT SEXUALITY/Integration Stage
• Self-oriented • Sexuality involves exploration of self, discovering what feels good physically.	• Self-oriented with another • Sexual acting out and seeking behavior with another, but disconnected emotionally.	• Other-oriented, sex is focused on connecting with another human being. • Sex is seen as but one part of a healthy, adult relationship.
Physical	**Physical-Fantasy**	**Emotional, Physical And Connected With Another**
— Exciting — Magical — Pleasurable — Nurturing — Purely physical — A time of discovery	— Exciting — Magical — Pleasurable — Fantasy — Beginning of dating relationships — Sexual acting out with others (kissing, petting, etc.) but, disconnected emotionally from other.	— Maturity — Healthy intimacy — Connected emotionally with sex partner — Sharing experience — Open communication — Pleasurable — Exciting
Natural, self-centered childhood immaturity, a time of physical self-discovery	Development of social skills and experimentation in opposite as well as same-sex relationships	A healthy sense of self allowing for individual differences and honest communication

Human beings develop in stages progressively, emotionally, physically, spiritually and sexually. Childhood abuse can stunt emotional, spiritual and sexual development. If one is abused sexually, during childhood, the abused individual may find himself or herself stuck in a particular stage of psychosexual development. The stage in which one becomes stuck relates to the stage of psychosexual development one was at during the time of the sexual abuse.

these issues were resolved, the relationship would be all right. In many cases problems with lack of communication, intimacy, sex, difficulties with children, job, money and in-laws result from some addictive dysfunction. For a relationship to heal, all addictive behaviors must be addressed, including sexual addiction. To succeed in having an intimate relationship with another human being, it is important for us as individuals to address all of our addictions and not enable those addictions that our partners have.

Have your partners, past or present, ever had you perform sexually in ways that made you feel uncomfortable? If so, please list these incidents.

a. _____
b. _____
c. _____
d. _____
e. _____

Is there anything you could have done to avoid participating in these uncomfortable sexual behaviors? List ways in which you could have said *no*.

a. _____
b. _____
c. _____
d. _____
e. _____

Did you fear not participating in these behaviors? If so, what were your fears about? _____

_____

Do you see yourself as being sexually abused by your partner? _____ Are your sexual needs being met by your partner? _____

Individuals who participate in sexual activities that they find emotionally or physically uncomfortable usually are the products of sexual abuse themselves. Sexually abused as children, they learned that they did not have a choice and, as a result, they learned how to survive the abusive incidents at the expense of childhood memory loss. These survivors do not understand what a healthy physical, sexual exchange is all about. Some see themselves as the total problem, believing their partner's sexual values and behaviors are the norm. If a particular sexual act feels emotionally or physically abusive, shameful or uncomfortable, there is a reason for this and it is our responsibility to say no. If we continue to participate in the act, we are not only being abused but we are also abusing ourselves. Healthy couples discuss all aspects of sexuality and take individual responsibility for themselves in the sexual relationship.

As mentioned, sexual addiction is the result of childhood sexual abuse. Sex becomes the drug of choice for covering up feelings of anger, grief, fear, boredom and loneliness. Sexual fantasy and acting out cheat one out of the life experience and leave feelings of emptiness and loneliness.

> If you are sexually addicted, list those behaviors or activities that you use as a part of your addiction (excessive fantasy, magazines, movies, masturbation, excessive sexual acting out within your relationship, extramarital emotional and/or sexual affairs).
>
> a. _____
> b. _____
> c. _____
> d. _____
>
> Do you believe your sex-addicted behavior is interfering in your current relationship? _____ Does your partner ever complain about your sexual behavior? If so, how? ____
> Do you believe your sex-addicted behavior is abusive emotionally, physically or sexually to your partner? _____
> If so, how? _____
> _____
>
> If you are married to or involved with a sex addict, what are you willing to do to take care of yourself and not enable the addiction?
>
> a. _____
> b. _____
> c. _____

By not enabling addictive behavior and by taking care of ourselves we are refusing responsibility for the addiction. Because we are not enabling, the addict eventually has to suffer the consequences of the addiction and pain brings the motivation to recover.

If you are a sex addict, food addict, alcohol addict, drug addict, work addict, or addicted at all — what are you willing to do about your addiction (seek professional help, attend 12-Step support groups such as Sexual Addicts Anonymous, Overeaters Anonymous, Alcoholics Anonymous)?

a. _____

b. _____

c. _____

By taking responsibility for our addictive behavior, we are taking care of ourselves. When we take care of ourselves we develop a sense of self-love and begin to fill the emptiness our early abuse experiences created. By being responsible for our addiction, we no longer have to abuse ourselves or others because we learn how to respect others and love ourselves. As addicts we have lived in shame with feelings of unworthiness and loneliness. We have used addiction to try to fill up the emptiness within but the pain only increased as our addiction progressed. This is why we need the help of others to assist us along the path of recovery. Working with a professional or with the aid of a support group gives us a chance to address our shame, pain, anger and loneliness in safe and supportive atmospheres. Sharing these feelings with those who understand helps us to see that we are not alone and that healing is possible. Initially, this sharing of ourselves is difficult but if we have the courage to be vulnerable and honest with others who understand, we will be well on our way to recovery as individuals. When we begin to recover as individuals, movement towards healthy intimacy with others will also begin.

9

The Joy Of Recovery

For Michael and me, individually and as a couple, our initial recovery was very painful. Our old relationship had to die a slow death before we could rebuild as a recovering couple. It took a while for us to understand that even though we had problems in our relationship, those problems were but symptoms of our unfinished business from the past. My personal ingrained dysfunction was already quite visible before Michael and I had a relationship and as I worked through my family of origin issues, it became clear that my own unfinished business was 50 percent responsible for the dysfunction in our relationship.

Today, there are several things we do to continue our recovery process, not only individually but also as a couple. Each of us is involved in our own separate recovery process. Rule number one is that it is not my responsibility to tell Michael how to work his recovery process, nor is it his job to tell me what I need to do for my recovery. This is not to say that Michael and I cannot each express our concerns about the relationship. We have a right to every one of our own perceptions and feelings but if either of us expects the other to change as a result of expressing those feelings, then we are not focusing on our own recovery program.

I believe that for a relationship to be truly intimate, both partners must be involved in the recovery process. If one partner is active in addiction or is not dealing with unresolved family of origin issues, the chances for healthy communication and honest intimacy are very limited. Those addictions that we do not address will build a wall between us. If we are living behind the wall of addiction we never experience the joys of healthy relationships with self, others or a Higher Power. Addiction isolates us from the life experience.

Recovery as a couple involves each partner taking individual responsibility for his or her addictions and unfinished business. It also requires individual participation in support groups, therapy and — in some cases — treatment. Only after this can a couple correct the dysfunction within the relationship. To attempt to do so beforehand would be a waste of time, energy and money.

Many therapists claim to do marriage or relationship counseling. If they do not urge each partner to address the individual addictions and unfinished business before attempting marital or relationship counseling, then therapy will only temporarily bandage the problems — which are only symptoms. Focusing on the dysfunctional symptoms in a relationship only distracts from the real core issues of addiction and unresolved original family conflicts.

Michael and I each had to recover individually before we could learn how to recover as a couple. Part of my individual recovery process was learning to have boundaries in order to take care of myself. I had to learn how to say no and be responsible for my behavior which set me up not to take care of myself as an adult. I was very needy and expected others to fill those needs for me. By expecting my needs to be taken care of by others, I was never able to experience the joy and satisfaction of healthy, adult self-sufficiency. My neediness promoted for me feelings of shame, inadequacy and low self-esteem. I had trouble saying no to the demands of others for fear of rejection. My abandonment fears prevented me from taking care of myself and as a result of not setting limits with others, I constantly felt taken advantage of or abused. I used giving in relationships to ensure that I would not be rejected or left alone. The price I paid was my sense of self. As I got to the root of my abandonment fears, I was able to start healing. By healing, I started to fill my emptiness and start taking care of myself in ways that allowed me to feel comfortable in setting limits with others. For years I had given away money, personal possessions, time, energy and more to gain acceptance. With recovery I discovered I did not have to give until it hurt to be loved and that I had to love myself before I could give in a healthy manner. This included giving in my relationship to Michael.

Michael's recovery process involved learning how to ask for help and support from others. He had to learn that it was appropriate and healing to be vulnerable at times. Michael was *need-less* and believed he could conquer everything by himself. As an adolescent he had participated in an Outward Bound program in Colorado which taught him how to live off the land. He would, on occasion, be dropped off in some desert for two weeks with a one-week supply of food; at other times, he would find himself up in the Rocky Mountains during a blizzard, building a snow cave to sleep in. He learned how to be too self-sufficient and in recovery this was hard to overcome. Whenever he was told to let go, he was baffled because he had grown up always being in control.

Several years ago, Michael and I were driving in California on our way to visit one of my sisters who was living up in the mountains in a small town called Felton. I was looking forward to visiting with her and her husband and spending time in the mountains. Michael and I had been driving around the city of Felton for some time and we kept circling a particular mountain over and over again. I kept wondering why Michael would not stop and ask for directions. After the third or fourth time around the same mountain, I calmly asked, "Why don't you stop the car and ask for directions?" Michael said, with control and confidence, "No, I can find it." Instead of saying, "All right then, *I* will ask for directions," I stuffed my feelings and raged inwardly, not understanding why he couldn't ask for help, knowing he was lost and not in control at all. Instead of taking care of my needs and asking for directions myself, I was waiting for him to do it and take care of me. My neediness for acceptance and fear of rejection forced me to sacrifice my self-esteem and enabled him to be need-less. Michael, on the other hand, knew he was in trouble but didn't know how to ask for help and was hoping I would just be quiet.

We were each trapped in our own dysfunctional survival skills left over from childhood and eventually focused on each other's behavior, not realizing that we were both equally responsible for being lost. I was telling him how improper it was for him not to ask for directions, not realizing that I had a choice and could ask for directions myself. The more I complained about his behavior, the quieter he became as he focused on my dysfunctional verbal nagging and shaming. I appeared irrational to him, complaining about his inability to ask for help and he shut me out, viewing me as just being out of control and over-reacting. The more irrational I became, the more in control he appeared, as he continued to drive around the same mountain

Finally, I remembered that I was in recovery and that I had a choice about taking care of myself. I asked him to stop the car and when he did, I walked to a gas station and asked for directions. Instead of continuing to wait for Michael to take care of me, I discovered I could take care of myself. We were three hours late arriving at my sister's house but I had learned a valuable lesson in being responsible. Today Michael asks for help and when he's lost is often the first to suggest pulling into a gas station to ask for directions. As he has said during workshops we do together on addictive relationships, "I learned that it makes life a lot easier at times to just admit powerlessness and ask for help."

Setting boundaries in my relationships, for me, involved learning how to be more responsible for my own needs, not expecting others always to take care of me. For Michael, setting healthy fluid boundaries involved removing the walls of total self-sufficiency and allowing others into his life. As I began taking more responsibility for myself, Michael began defocusing off me, affirming that I am a competent adult woman, capable of taking care of my own needs. For years Michael had told me I needed to become more self-sufficient but each time he told me this I became more needy, fearing he would abandon me if I were self-sufficient. Michael was also invested in my being needy because it kept him from focusing on himself. As I set more boundaries by making healthy choices and decisions in my life, Michael began focusing more on his own recovery.

Being responsible for self in a healthy way is a hard task because most of us have grown up believing that either we are responsible only to others at the expense of ourselves or only to ourselves at the expense of others. We grew up with extreme behaviors so we view our relationships and the world around us also in the extreme. Recovery means learning to live with *balance* in our attitudes and our behaviors. Recovery is knowing that as individuals we are all unique, special, worthwhile and deserving of love and appreciation and at the same time we need to respect, appreciate and support one another. We are independent beings while at the same time interdependent on one another for the survival of our species and planet. Pia Melody, a nationally known speaker in the field of addictions and the family of origin recovery process, has stated that the core of dysfunctional boundaries are unresolved abuse issues. She has further stated that abused children grow up to be dysfunctional adults who cannot take care of themselves in a healthy manner as a result of their dysfunctional boundaries. In order to develop healthy boundaries for ourselves and in our relationships with others, we must begin with our own personal healing process. As we learn how to heal ourselves with the help of support groups, therapy or treatment, we start to develop healthy boundaries which spill out into our relationships with others.

The All Rights

Some healthy boundaries form in a recovering relationship as a result of individual healing. The following are some of them.

It Is All Right To Disagree With Our Spouse, Lover, Friends, Family And Children

So many of us have always believed that disagreement and confrontation are unacceptable. We have believed that to disagree about issues or to have differing opinions was somehow discourteous or inappropriate. In dysfunctional families it is not acceptable to be an individual — being an individual would be to not accept or to go against the family. When we grow up, we either sacrifice our own opinions to agree with others, out of fear of rejection — or we want others to always agree with us, so we can feel validated about ourselves. This family prohibition to being an individual stunts honest, open communication and intimacy. It is all right to disagree with one another within a relationship. It does not mean that we dislike one another. To disagree can promote healthy intimacy.

It Is All Right To Ask For Personal And Emotional Space

People need a balance of time alone and time spent with others. When we spend all our time surrounded by others or in complete isolation we are living in the world of extremes. It is important to balance time spent with self and time spent with others.

Many of us were taught to fear being all alone or to fear being vulnerable with other people. We learned that we were accepted if we were there for others. Our self-worth came only from doing for others and as adults we have no sense of self. We never were able to develop our inner self and the thought of being alone causes intense fear of abandonment. To heal, we must learn how to be by ourselves and nurture ourselves. We need to learn how to feel complete within instead of depending on others to make us feel complete.

For those of us who fear others because of our own shame and lack of trust, it is important to explore the family of origin issues which set us up to feel safe only when we are alone.

In a healthy family, individuals learn to balance time alone with time spent with others. Many of us have remained in emotionally, physically, even sexually abusive relationships out of fear of being alone. Some of us fear sharing ourselves completely with others because we fear being abandoned or abused and we isolate ourselves to be safe. In wholesome relationships, time is spent together and apart on a regular basis. Asking for emotional or physical space does not always imply rejection or lack of love. It can just mean that we or our partners need some time for self. Asking for space promotes self-nurturing. Spending quality time with others promotes trust. Both alone time and time spent with others encourage the development of healthy intimacy.

It Is All Right To Leave An Issue Or Problem Temporarily Unresolved

Many of us grew up in environments where either there was never any obvious conflict or there was always chaotic conflict. As a result, we may be uncomfortable with conflict and either over-react or under-react. We have a strong need for control because being in control allowed us to survive. Our need for control also requires immediate resolution of even those difficult issues that confront us in adult life and gaining immediate resolution may produce a solution that is inappropriate or not well thought out — or it may involve avoidance of the conflict or problem altogether.

Few of us have the tools for healthy problem-solving and we rarely resolve our conflicts fully. Because it is so hard for us to deal with the feelings of anxiety, fear, anger, pain and grief which are associated with conflict, we look for quick fixes to alleviate or avoid these feelings. Usually, healthy problem-solving requires time for exploration of not just one solution but several. It takes feeling all the feelings associated with the problem that confronts us and this, too, takes time. If we do not allow ourselves the time for problem-solving and we look for a quick fix, the same problem will eventually face us again in the future, perhaps disguised as a different problem but in reality, the same old unresolved issue.

Most couples disagree over and over again about the same issues within their relationship because they do not know how to feel feelings, discuss options and experiment with implementing those options; even then, that may not be enough time.

It Is All Right To Go To Bed Angry

Whenever I hear someone say, "My partner and I never go to bed angry," I immediately suspect distress in the relationship. Individuals in intimate relationships do become angry with one another from time to time; it's a natural consequence of being in a close connection with another human being. Resolving angry conflict is an individual experience for each partner. What happens if the issue cannot be resolved before bed? Usually, it is never resolved; it is pushed underground. Many couples in therapy have admitted to using sex as a making-up technique after a disagreement, but when asked if the sexual encounter resolved the problem, most replied no, stating that eventually the same unresolved conflict re-emerges. The belief that sex and intimacy are the same thing — if you have sex with me, that means you love me or, only during sexual encounters do I feel intimate with my partner — is common among individuals who do not understand intimacy. Sex can appear to be a temporary bandage for problems in a realtionship but in reality, it only complicates matters. Sex can temporarily distance us from our problems but it does not solve them. Going to bed angry is very acceptable because it can provide the emotional and, in some cases, the physical space we need to examine our disagreements.

It's All Right To Have Hobbies And Interests Apart From Your Partner

Michael loves golf. I dislike it. I have no interest in chasing a small white ball across sand traps and acres of green grass. I thought for many years that since we were partners in a relationship it was my job to learn how to play and enjoy golf as much as he does. The harder I tried to like the game, the more resentful I became of golf balls, clubs, gloves, tees and players. I like opera. Michael finds it boring. We bought season tickets to the opera one year. Every time we went, Michael would do one of two things: He would either get sleepy or continually ask when we could leave — before the opera was over. "Can we leave during the intermission?" Michael thought he had to learn to love opera as much as I do.

Today, we know it's okay for us to have our individual likes and dislikes. Michael still plays golf and I still listen to opera. I don't play golf and Michael continues to have little interest in opera. What makes a relationship interesting is the individual differences of each partner. This is what makes us unique. Accepting individual differences promotes continual growth for ourselves, our partners and the relationship. Partners need time away from each other pursuing interests outside of the relationship. Once again, it is important to have a balance of time for the relationship and for individual hobbies and activities outside of the relationship. Too little time or too much time in the relationship stunts not only personal growth, but also intimacy.

It Is All Right To Have Different Friends

For many years Michael and I had the same friends. It never occurred to me that I could have a friend who was not also a friend of Michael's. In dysfunctional family systems, many of us learned early that we could only have those friends of whom parents approved. If our parents were prejudiced against a particular race, creed, religion or economic status, this influenced our selection of friends. We may have complied with their desire for us to associate with certain friends or we may have rebelled by selecting friends that our parents would surely disapprove of. We carry these behaviors into our relationships in adulthood. We may only associate with those individuals that our partners approve of or we may associate with those our partners disapprove of in order to get a reaction or as a means of rebelling. We may find we really do not have many friends except for our partner's friends. It was important for me to find women friends to whom I could relate and it was also important for Michael to find a group of male friends that he felt comfortable with. Many of us have difficulty feeling comfortable with members of the same sex because of a lack of appropriate parenting from our same-sex parent. Some of us may feel it is easier to share with members of the opposite sex. This, too, is a consequence of a lack of healthy parenting from our opposite-sex parent. Same-sex parents in a healthy family teach us how to have healthy intimate friendships with same

sex individuals. If our same-sex parent was addicted or dysfunctional in any way, chances are they were not at ease with
themselves and so incapable of modeling for us how to have
healthy, same-sex relationships. If our opposite-sex parent was
emotionally unavailable due to addiction or dysfunction, we
did not receive all the parenting and nurturing to teach us how
to have healthy relationships with members of the opposite
sex. We may be needy for attention from members of the
opposite sex as a result of never receiving enough healthy
affirmation from our opposite-sex parent and find that we
cross over into emotional or physical affairs in order to fulfill
this need for opposite-sex parenting.

Friends are important and we need healthy friendships
outside of our intimate relationships. If the intimacy needs
within the relationship are being taken care of by someone
outside the relationship, the relationship is in trouble. Healthy
friendships encourage growth and offer support and are necessary in or out of a significant relationship.

It Is All Right Not To Like Your Mate's Behavior

*His behavior doesn't bother me. We have never had a fight.
How could I ever be upset with her?* These comments indicate
that a relationship lacks intimacy, honest communication and
life. We think we have to like or learn to like everything about
our partner. We believe that if we don't like something about
our partner, we just have to learn to live with it or accept it. To
accept, for many of us, means to ignore, to avoid or to act as
if there is no problem. This is denial. "I do not have to accept
unacceptable behavior" is a quote I have heard from many
recovering individuals and one I believe in personally. It is all
right to not like our partner's behavior, haircut, language, style
of dress, addictions, parents, friends, hobbies, car, hygiene
standards or whatever. It is also all right to express the way we
feel about what we do not like. "Michael, I feel angry when
you do not put the lid on the jam and put it away after using
it for breakfast." Putting things away has always been a big
issue for us and for years, instead of talking about our feelings
regarding behavior, we would both stuff our feelings and try
to ignore our irritation with one another. Eventually we would

have one big fight and every unexpressed issue we each had stored up over a period of months would emerge all at once.

Many of us grew up hearing, "If you can't say something nice, don't say anything at all," and we have difficulty expressing our feelings as they come up about those things we find unacceptable. It is appropriate to state how we feel about what we see going on with our partners but to expect change as a result of what we have said is usually a setup for disappointment. When Michael says, "Carla, I get really angry when you park your car so close to mine," he is making the statement to me for himself. He is emotionally taking care of himself by stating how he feels about my behavior. By the way, I still park my car too close to his on occasion but when he states how he feels about it, he feels better for taking care of himself by expressing his feelings. Expressing feelings as they come up in a relationship clears the air and promotes healthy, open communication. Keeping feelings from one another builds resentments and perpetuates distrust.

It's All Right To Have Separate Territories

One of the first things Michael and I did as a recovering couple was to open separate checking accounts. We were so focused on each other, or, as psychotherapists say, enmeshed, that neither of us knew where the other ended and we, as individuals, began.

My closet was also a source of disagreement for years. Throughout our relationship, my closet periodically becomes impossible to get into. I have clothes strewn in piles all over the floor and sometimes they appear to be creeping out of the closet. We referred to the disaster in my closet as "the creature." At times Michael would go into my closet to straighten it up. Afterward I would not be able to find a thing. Instead of expressing my feelings about this, I would stuff them. I knew Michael was trying to help and I feared sharing with him how upset I really was when he went into my closet and moved things around. My sloppy system worked for me and each time he would organize it the way he thought it should be, I was an emotional wreck because I couldn't find anything. It was my responsibility to set limits and boundaries in our relationship by saying, "Please stay out of my closet."

It is important to respect one another's personal belongings and private items. It is also important to speak up and communicate with one another when we feel we are not being respected or, in some cases, violated with regard to our personal space and belongings. Mind-reading does not work in a relationship and, in the long run, expectation of it causes extreme misunderstanding and difficulty between partners in a relationship.

It Is All Right To Say No To Or Disagree With Our Family Of Origin And In-laws

One of the issues most couples have disagreements about regularly is family, be it family of origin members or in-laws. Since most of us come from families which were dysfunctional during our childhood, it would only make sense to assume that without recovery or intervention, our family of origin will continue to be dysfunctional during our adult life. We have heard the saying, "You are marrying me, not my family, so stop worrying." Since we are all a product of our family of origin to one extent or another, we are going to have disagreements with our partners that are rooted in unresolved family of origin business. It is important to understand this concept, otherwise we will experience the same troubles our parents had in their relationships. We may be fighting our parents' unresolved battles.

Setting limits and boundaries with our family of origin and in-laws can be very hard to do because it may mean a change in behavior — usually, saying no. We may also fight over our partner's behavior toward our family of origin, fearing how our mate's actions will affect our relationship with them. Sometimes we may expect our partner to be a buffer between us and our family by keeping peace, being silent about or complying with the dysfunction within our original family. How often I have heard, "If only his family would . . ." or, "I wish her family would . . ." from couples who are having problems in their relationship. Focusing on and addressing unresolved issues about the families of origin usually resolved these difficulties. It is also all right for our partner to have his or her own opinions about our family. For us to have expectations as to how they should behave in family situations is a setup for disagreement and resentment. If our partner complies with our expectations for his behavior toward our family, he may also be enabling the dysfunction and buffering us from the distress we need to see in order to deal with our pain about the past. If we focus on our partner's behavior towards our family, this keeps us from seeing those issues that need to be resolved by us vis-a-vis our family of origin.

It Is All Right To Say No To Sex
And It Is All Right To Talk About Sex

A sexual encounter between two people within a relationship is a two-way street. Both partners are responsible for setting limits and asking for what they need during the encounter. I hear comments such as, "I really don't like it when . . ." or "I wish she (or he) would do more of . . ." during discussions about sexual difficulty within a relationship. When I ask if these issues were discussed with the partner, the answer is usually no. For most of us in the family sex was not discussed in an open manner while growing up, and if we were sexually abused we have little understanding of what appropriate sexual behavior is. Sex is confused with intimacy and in many instances, there is the myth that the more intense the sexual encounter is, the more in love are the partners and intimate the relationship. If the sexual relationship is based on sexual addiction where there is either too little or too much of a sexual demand, the relationship is void of true intimacy. In a sexual relationship it is important to discuss likes and dislikes with regards to the physical, sexual aspect of the relationship. If the encounter brings feelings of aloneness, anger, emptiness, fear or shame for one or both partners, the sexual relationship is probably dysfunctional and based on sexual addiction. When we do not wish to have sex with our partner or when we feel uncomfortable participating in particular sexual acts, it is our responsibility to take care of ourselves and say no. If we are concerned over a lack of sexual activity, it is also our responsibility to speak up and share our concerns. For those of us who have used sex as the only means of connecting with our partner, it is important to begin exploring why this is and what needs to change to promote other avenues for connecting which will encourage healthy intimacy. I have heard couples say, "We have a hard time talking with one another but our sex life makes up for all of that," or "We have a whole bunch of unresolved problems but we still have a great relationship because we have great sex." Sex, though an important part of a relationship, is just that — only a part. When there is sexual addiction in a relationship, it is important for both partners to seek help through SAA, CoSA, therapy and, in some cases, treatment. With outside help, couples can slowly begin rebuilding the dysfunctional relationship. At times, it may be important to abstain from sexual acting out altogether for a period of time so that true intimacy can be developed between the partners.

Learning how to be friends again is important for couples recovering from the complications that sexual addiction can bring. The process of developing healthy intimacy takes time, depending on the amount of resentment in need of resolution. Painful feelings on both sides need healing and it is important not to rush the recovery process as this will only sabotage the potential for a healthy relationship in the long run. Usually trust has been lost and healthy communication is gone by the time a couple realizes that the relationship is in trouble. Recovery from any addiction being acted out in a relationship causes anguish and attaining it takes dedication and courage on the part of both partners.

Setting up sexual boundaries, rebuilding communication and trust provide the foundation for a healthy relationship. Initially it may appear that there is more disagreement going on than before and that things are getting worse. In reality, this is a healthy sign because during this time issues are being resolved and boundaries are being set. This involves trial and error and conflict. It also indicates that both partners are taking care of themselves. Eventually, the conflict in the relationship levels out as a new and exciting relationship based on healthy intimacy emerges.

It Is All Right To Have Fun In A Relationship

Michael and I did not know how to have fun in our relationship and we didn't even know that this is a part of the rebuilding process for an intimate relationship. Couples need to take a break now and then from the intensity of the healing process to learn how to enjoy each other and play. Some couples have a date night once a week when they go away from the problems in the relationship for a short time to just enjoy each other. In our case, Michael and I had rarely taken vacations because we were both fearful of spending much time together. Initially in our recovery, we began taking weekend trips alone together to the seashore or the hill country to get reacquainted with one another. At first it was hard because we had to *talk to one another.* There wasn't anything to distract us from our relationship and we had to work on communicating. Eventually, we began enjoying each other and today we often take small trips for the sheer pleasure of having fun together. We also have a date night each week when we spend time as a couple doing something enjoyable. One week Michael is responsible for planning our date while the following week, the way we spend our night out is up to me. We have had some new experiences together and experimented with different leisure activities during our recovery. Playtime together brings a break of lightness into the relationship during the healing process. It is important to remember that we are never too old to play and that learning how to enjoy life is part of the healing process.

Conclusion

I believe life is supposed to be a journey during which we grow and develop into the spiritual being we are each destined to be — like a training ground where we learn about ourselves in relation to the world and those around us. I also believe our relationships teach us about ourselves and that is why they are so important.

John Bradshaw has said in his book, *Bradshaw On: The Family*, that 96 percent of the families in this country suffer from one type of dysfunction or another. As a result, we live in a world with others who are operating with the dysfunctional survival skills learned while growing up in the families of origin.

Recently I was at the local deli getting some lunch when the above fact was brought home to me on a personal level. Standing in line waiting to pay for my lunch, I heard a loud "Uh, hum!" followed by an angry and undignified, "Excuse me!" I was confronted by a very angry woman who flashed

me a shaming look, as if I had offended her. With the skills of
a survivor from a dysfunctional family, the first thing I thought
was "Oh, no! What did I do to this poor woman to make her
so angry with me?" Well, I had done nothing to her but being
a shame-based individual, I thought her anger was my fault.
In reality the woman was angry that I did not see her and did
not move so she could reach the potato chips. She also might
have been angry because of some incident at work or she
may have been upset over something in a significant relationship. She was most likely operating on her own family of
origin survival skills and I was reacting to her as I had in my
own original family. Our pasts were being acted out. I believe
this kind of situation occurs on a regular basis for most, if not
all, of us in our relationships with others.

The incident brought back to me again how, in our society
as a whole, we act out of our family of origin with one another
and that this causes much misunderstanding and confusion
for us on the job, with friends, family and our children.

I also believe that our unresolved original family issues
affect our country's politics and attitudes toward other coun-
tries. As a society, we do not know how to communicate with
one another in effective, healthy ways. I believe the lack of
healthy communication and understanding between people,
along with the tremendous lack of respect for self and others,
is partly responsible for the wars, pollution, inner isolation
and aloneness that are so prevalent on our planet today.

Healing begins with the self. It is always primary. As we
heal from our own addictions and unfinished business with
the help of support groups, recovering friends and family,
caring teachers and therapists, we can also begin to heal our
relationships. I have seen the domino effect of the healing
process, both personally and professionally, with couples and
with entire families. I have had the pleasure of watching
individuals find themselves and then move on toward healing
their relationships. We do not, as some have put it, have to be
slaves to our addictions and families of origin. If we are
willing to work hard, we can slowly free ourselves from the
unhealthy chains that bind us to the shame we carry within.
It takes courage and is painful at times to cut ourselves free

from the bonds of the past but it is also an exciting adventure. It is living life to the fullest and evolving into the intuitive, creative, spiritual beings we are meant to be. The healing process is not something to be avoided but to be embraced.

This book is only meant to be a beginning. I do not claim to have all the answers and hope that these pages will be looked upon by you, the reader, as only an initial guide. We all have the answers to the many questions within us, waiting to be acknowledged. It is my hope that, as they say in 12-Step support groups, you will "take what you like and leave the rest." We are all individuals and what has worked for me may or may not work for you. I do hope, for those of you who have done me the honor of reading my book, that you will be encouraged to continue seeking your own answers. If my work has provided for you the motivation to either begin or continue your own journey, then I have done what I set out to do.

I wish you success in your personal journey and in healing your relationships with others.

Suggested Reading

Baldwin, Martha. **You Can Overcome Childhood Abuse; Even Sexual Abuse.** Moore Haven, FL: Rainbow Books, 1988.

Bradshaw, John. **Bradshaw On: The Family.** Deerfield Beach, FL: Health Communications, 1988.

_____. **Healing The Shame That Binds You.** Deerfield Beach, FL: Health Communications, 1989.

Carnes, Patrick. **Out Of The Shadows: Understanding Sexual Addiction.** Minneapolis, MN: Comp Care, 1983.

Hope And Recovery: A Guide For Healing From Compulsive Sexual Behavior. Minneapolis, MN: Comp Care, 1987.

Sex And Love Addicts Anonymous, **The Basic Text For The Augustine Fellowship.** Boston: Sex and Love Addicts Anonymous, Fellowship-Wide Services, 1986.

Subby, Robert. **Lost In The Shuffle, The Co-dependent Reality.** Pompano Beach, FL: Health Communications, 1987.

Utain, Marcia and Barbara Oliver. **Scream Louder: Through Hell And Healing With An Incest Survivor And Her Therapist.** Deerfield Beach, FL: Health Communications, 1989.

Wills-Brandon, Carla. **Eat Like A Lady: Guide For Overcoming Bulimia.** Deerfield Beach, FL: Health Communications, 1989.

Woititz, Janet Geringer. **Healing Your Sexual Self.** Deerfield Beach, FL: Health Communications, 1989.

Appendix:
Support Groups

Co-dependents Anonymous
Central Office
P.O. Box 5508
Glendale, Arizona 85312-5508
(602) 944-0141

Sex and Love Addicts Anonymous
The Augustine Fellowship
Fellowship-Wide Services, Inc.
P.O. Box 119, New Town Branch
Boston, Massachusetts 02258

Sexual Addicts Anonymous
Twin Cities Sexual Addicts Anonymous
P.O. Box 3038
Minneapolis, Minnesota 55403

CoSA (Co-dependents on Sexual Addicts)
Twin Cities CoSA
P.O. Box 14537
Minneapolis, Minnesota 55414

Sexaholics Anonymous
P.O. Box 300
Simi Valley, California 93062

Sexual Abuse Anonymous
P.O. Box 80085
Minneapolis, Minnesota 55408
(612) 251-4357

Survivors of Incest Anonymous
P.O. Box 21817
Baltimore, Maryland 21222
(301) 282-3400

Printed in the United States
1540100001B/264